Successful Diabetes Management

Photo by Joanna Hays

Lloyd Mann

First Edition

Copyright © 2011 by Lloyd Mann

All rights reserved.

No part of this book may be reproduced in any form or by any electronic or mechanical means including information storage and retrieval systems, without permission in writing from the author. The only exception is by a reviewer, who may quote short excerpts in a review.

Printed in the United States of America

First Printing: May 2011

ISBN-13: 978-1461143550

Dedication

To Richard, who paved the way, and without whose encouragement, this book might never have happened.

Forward

My intent is to inform, in such a way as to assist without overwhelming. For the most part, this is written for the newly diagnosed, but I would like to think that in 17 years I have picked up some tidbits of knowledge that would be useful to a large number of diabetics. We never stop learning, just when we think we have diabetes figured out, we get knocked for a loop by the unexpected.

Table of Contents

What is Diabetes..........................1
Metabolic Syndrome........................5
Dawn Phenomenon and Somogyi Effect........7
The Vicious Cycle........................10
That's My Story and I am Sticking To It..12
My 15 Minutes of Fame....................19
Just Diagnosed?..........................21
Diabetes Management......................22
Tools for Success........................28
Your Professional Team...................30
Internet Resources.......................31
Attitude is Paramount....................34
Take Ownership of your Diabetes..........36
Frequent Problems........................38
Know Thyself.............................40
Diet and Exercise........................41
How to Count Carbohydrates...............43
Oral Medications (pills).................46
Peptide Analogs (injectables)............48

```
Insulin........................................48
Glucose Meter.................................50
Continuous Glucose Monitor...............52
Using Insulin................................55
An Insulin Pen...............................58
An Insulin Pump..............................59
Pumping Tips.................................60
Pump Batteries...............................65
Infusion Sets................................66
Making Pump Adjustments..................78
Standard Deviation.........................80
Blood Tests..................................81
My Well Rested Pancreas..................85
Medical Exams...............................89
Will my Diabetes get Worse?.............90
Travel........................................92
Future Technologies........................95
Low Carbohydrate Treats..................96
Frequently Asked Questions..............98
```

What is Diabetes?

In a non-diabetic person with a pancreas that is working normally, carbohydrates eaten get digested, and enter the bloodstream as glucose, a form of sugar. Your body senses this, and the beta cells of your pancreas produce a hormone called insulin, which allows the cells all over your body to absorb the glucose for energy. Your pancreas sits behind your stomach. One of the tasks of your liver is to absorb glucose when you eat, and release it slowly into your bloodstream between meals to provide you with a continuous source of energy.

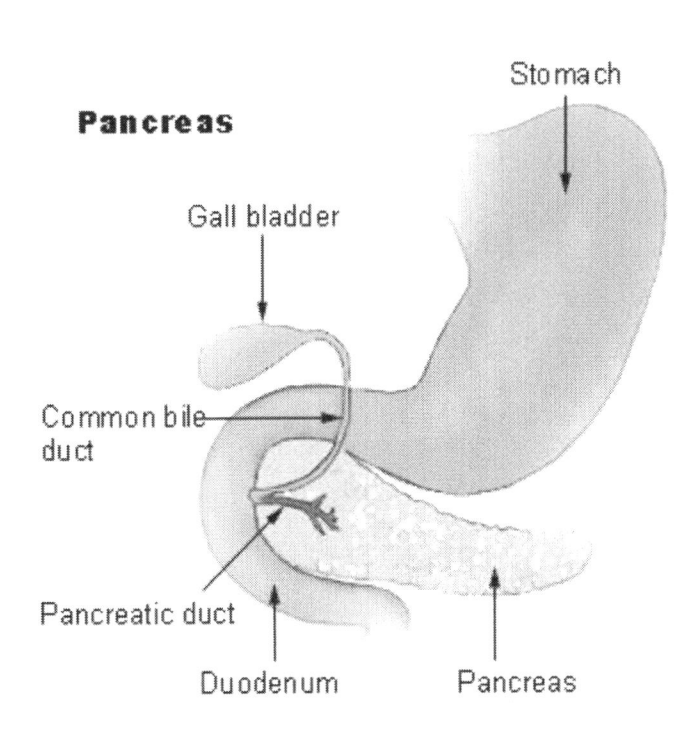

Type 1 diabetes is an auto immune problem. While fighting a virus or similar problem, the immune system can on rare occasions attack the beta cells of a pancreas, killing these cells. These are the cells that produce insulin. At that point, a person needs to inject insulin or infuse it with an insulin pump, otherwise they would have a life expectancy of less than 2 years. Type 1 used to be called juvenile diabetes, or insulin dependent diabetes, neither of which is very accurate. Anyone can get type 1 at any age. Common perception is that only young people can get type 1 diabetes, but more adults are diagnosed with type 1 (and 1.5) than younger people. Other types of diabetics use insulin and are dependent on it, so "insulin dependent" is not a good name either. Insulin dependent could be type 1 or type 2.

Type 2 diabetes is all about the inability to use insulin efficiently, and about relative shortages of insulin. Insulin is made by our pancreas (we have only one). It starts out with a reserve capacity, and can make more insulin than we need. If we lose the ability to use insulin efficiently, we are said to have insulin resistance. We can have resistance and not know it, as long as our body can still make enough insulin to keep our glucose at acceptable levels. When our need for insulin increases beyond the capacity of our pancreas to produce it, the amount of glucose in our blood increases.

At that point, symptoms may be present, and the rise in glucose can be measured. This is the first indication most people have that there is a problem. Symptoms vary, but the most common are excessive thirst, hunger, and urination. Exercise helps lower our blood glucose and reduces insulin resistance. Eating fewer carbohydrates decreases the amount of insulin needed.

Pills and injectable medicines help reduce our resistance, slow our digestion, regulate how much glucose our liver produces, or induce our pancreas to produce more insulin. These medicines are taken in combination, as needed.

Type 2 is said to be progressive, that means as time goes on your pancreas makes less and less insulin. This also means that more has to be done to keep your glucose at acceptable levels. This may involve more exercise, eating fewer carbohydrates, higher doses of the medications you are taking and additional medications.

Usually at some point diet, exercise, pills and other injectables no longer provide enough help. It's not that they don't work any more, it's just that your pancreas can no longer produce enough insulin even with their help.

At that point, it is time to take insulin. Type 2's often take slow acting insulin, once or twice a day, this is called basal insulin. This seems to be enough for about half of the type 2's that try it. It lowers your glucose, but still requires your pancreas to help out at mealtimes.

If you need more help than that, sometimes you are put on an insulin that is a mixture of slow and fast acting insulin. This also involves 2 injections a day, at mealtimes. While this can provide better results, for it to work right you need to eat the same amount of carbohydrates every day, and at the same time. You are matching your food to your insulin.

A more flexible and accurate way is to take fast acting insulin (called Bolus) with each meal, and Basal insulin once or twice a day. This is called MDI (Multiple Daily Injections) or B & B (Basal and Bolus). The amount of bolus is varied to match the amount of carbohydrates you eat.

Another way of delivering insulin is by way of an insulin pump. Fast acting insulin in small amounts is continuously delivered and a larger amount of fast acting is delivered when you eat. A pump does not think for itself, you have to tell it what insulin you want delivered. You do this ahead of time. The pump stores instructions, and once it is adjusted properly, so that it knows how many carbohydrates get one unit of insulin, you then only need to tell it when you are about to eat (and how many grams of carbohydrate you will be eating), and the pump takes care of the rest.

In some situations a pump is much better than injections. For example, when you need very small amounts of insulin, and when the amount of insulin you need varies by time of day, independent of what you eat.

Not all type 2 diabetics are overweight, about 20 percent are not. For the rest, weight is a problem, often a lifelong challenge. Arguably, we can discuss whether insulin resistance comes first or being overweight comes first, but in the long run it really does not matter. Both things happen, and each makes the other worse. Current studies have revealed that part of the cause of type 2 is an autoimmune reaction, and part of the reason is genetic.

Double diabetes is the informal, but widely accepted term for people who have almost no insulin production, while at the same time having significant insulin resistance. They have all the problems a type 1 has, and at least some of the problems a type 2 has, hence the name. Officially, it is type 1 with insulin resistance. You treat the insulin resistance, as a type 2 would. First choice would usually be Metformin. Actos is also available, if a person has adverse side effects from metformin that don't go away. In addition, you treat with insulin, as a type 1 would.

The most common way for this to happen is for a type 1 to gain significant weight, often due to medications such as steroids, or untreated thyroid problems. A type 2 can also have an autoimmune attack, and become type 1 almost overnight, though this does not seem to happen as often. This is also called type 1 with insulin resistance. If extra weight is lost, the insulin resistance may go down to the point where it no longer needs to be treated.

Metabolic Syndrome

A name has been given to a combination of medical disorders, called Metabolic Syndrome

The list of disorders varies a little depending on who is doing the defining, but a typical list is:

- Central Obesity, waist measurement greater than 40 inches for males and greater than 36 inches for females, or a BMI (Body Mass Index) greater than 30
- Triglycerides greater than 150
- HDL less than 40 in males and less than 50 in females
- Blood pressure greater than 130 systolic or greater than 85 diastolic, or previously diagnosed hypertension
- Fasting plasma glucose greater than 100 or previously diagnosed type 2

These are warning signs of increased risk of diabetes, if not already diagnosed, and of heart problems. You don't need to have all of these symptoms to have Metabolic Syndrome. It is highly debated whether in this case, the whole is greater than the sum of it's parts, or whether the whole is exactly equal to the sum of its parts.

That these things are not good, is not disputed. You can tackle them one at a time, or work on all of them. The better you do with the weight control, the easier it is to control the others. Very often, metabolic syndrome leads to type 2 diabetes. You can avoid future problems by working with your doctor to treat these symptoms.

Dawn Phenomenon and Somogyi Effect

What is the difference?
Both result in a higher glucose reading in the morning, but they have different causes and different treatments. Dawn phenomenon is caused by a release of growth hormones, cortisol, glucagon and epinephrine that increase insulin resistance, according to the Mayo Clinic. Somogyi effect is caused by an overnight low, which results in a release of glucose by the liver, (glycogen), which in turn causes high blood sugar in the morning. Your body is overreacting to low blood sugar.

Dawn Phenomenon
One of the things an insulin pump can do really well, is counteract the affects of Dawn Phenomenon. With an insulin pump, you can have a multitude of changing basal rates, to change the amount of insulin you get during the night. You develop the rates by trial and error, the use of a continuous glucose monitor makes this much easier and more quickly done, but you can do it without it

In my case I need 6 times as much insulin at 3:00 AM as 3:00 PM.

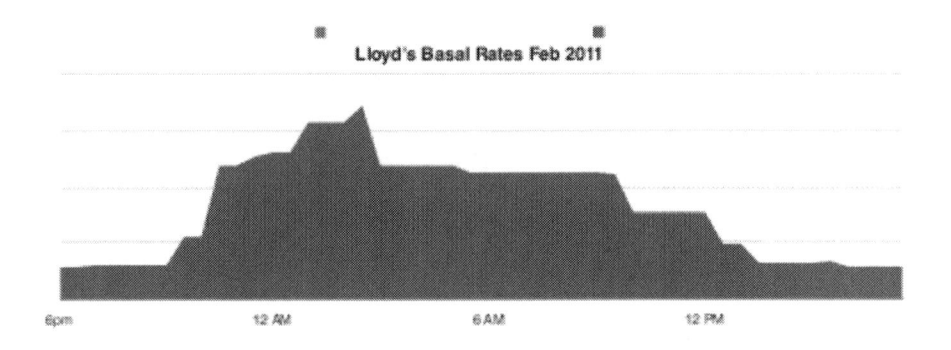

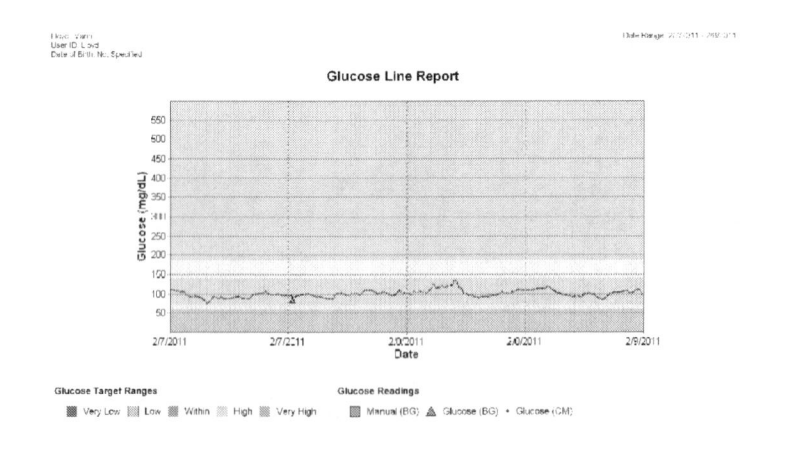

Somogyi Effect, AKA Rebound

The trick to taking care of Somogyi Effect is to prevent the low that causes the rebound. Before bed, you have a snack of something that digests slowly. Many people have found that peanut butter works very well for this. If you prevent the low, you prevent the rebound.

The Vicious Cycle

Type 2 diabetes usually involves resistance to the hormone insulin. This hormone allows the cells of your body to absorb the glucose in your bloodstream, which is needed for energy. When you don't have enough energy, you often don't feel like taking part in physical activity. Also when you don't get enough energy you get hungry again, not all that long after eating. So you eat more and exercise less. Part of the excess glucose in your bloodstream is converted to fat. Gaining weight tends to increase our insulin resistance, and decrease our activity level. This is the vicious cycle. Breaking the cycle is very hard for most of us. How do you loose weight when you are always hungry? Many of us need help.

For some a drug like Byetta can, among other things, reduce your appetite.

For others, insulin in the correct amount by way of injection or insulin pump is the answer.

For all, some kind of exercise at least 5 days a week will help.

Carbohydrates in food are primarily what gets converted to glucose (sugar) which ends up in your bloodstream. If you limit the amount of carbohydrates, you will limit the amount of glucose in your bloodstream.

Also, if you are taking insulin you need to know how many grams of carbohydrates you are eating so you can take the correct amount of insulin your body needs to process those carbohydrates. Too much insulin means your blood will contain too little glucose (a low), too little insulin means too much glucose, (a high). Both can and will hurt you.

Being good at counting carbohydrates is an extremely important skill for any diabetic to have.

Type 2 Diabetes is progressive. At first, diet and exercise may keep it in check. If you can avoid gaining weight, or loose weight if that is needed, you can stop the progression in its tracks. You may stop it for a while, or a long while, or in rare cases perhaps for the rest of your life if the problem is taken care of soon enough.

One of the functions of your liver is to store glucose like a sponge when you eat, and release it later a little at a time to help tide you over until the next meal, even if that means until the next morning.

Oral medications (pills) help by making you more sensitive to the insulin you produce, to slow down digestion so that the buildup of glucose in your blood happens more slowly. They reduce the amount of glucose that your liver releases in a given time, or induce your pancreas to produce more insulin.

These are all good things to do to help you avoid the complications from diabetes which are the result of blood sugar being too high. Most of these medicines can lead to weight gain. Metformin does not, which is one reason it is usually the first one they give you.

Some of the medicines carry some risk of making your blood glucose go too low. These are called Sulfonylureas, they get your pancreas to increase its insulin production. Most type 2's can feel it if their glucose is too low, and testing by a glucose meter will show if this is the case.

Because we have a resistance to insulin, most T2's need more insulin than a person without diabetes does. What happens is, at some point, our pancreas just can't produce enough insulin to satisfy our needs. When that happens, our blood glucose goes high and never really comes back down to where it needs to be, until medication or insulin brings it down.

That's My Story and I'm Sticking to It!

I'll start 30 years ago, when I got sick. My food would not digest properly, and I would end up staying up awake half the night with stomach problems. I went to the doctor and explained my problem, and that this had been getting progressively worse. I had blood tests, and drank barium for an upper GI scope that followed. The next day was the office visit. The doctor said, "We have found the problem, you just have to take this tiny pill every day for the rest of your life." It only costs a penny! That was then, this is now. That 1¢ pill now costs 36¢. The pill was Synthroid, and the problem was I had become hypothyroid. My thyroid gland was working so poorly that my entire digestive system and metabolism was slowed way down. Synthroid is a wonder drug, no doubt about it. I went from feeling like I would trip on the cracks of a sidewalk, to feeling like I could jump over parked cars! After a while that settled down, and I just felt normal. Yearly testing was done, and the dosage changed, they even have the pills color coded by dosage. About 10 years later my thyroid gave up completely, that made things easier as the dosage has remained steady since then.

About the time my thyroid gave up the ghost, a sibling was in the hospital for extremely high triglycerides, over 1000. They tested our parents and all the siblings. My triglyceride reading was 366 (it should be under 150), this was beyond the ninety-ninth percentile. Others in my family had triglyceride problems to lesser degrees. So, it was time to take niacin. Yikes, I hated that stuff, it turned my skin orange. As time went on I went from one medication to another, triglyceride readings of about 200 was the best I could do. This was treated by an endocrinologist, who became my regular doctor. This worked out well, as I don't get sick very often.

As I got older, I began to put on weight. I really didn't think all that much about it. Then one spring, at age 44, my doctor said I had diabetes. I had developed some of the classic symptoms of type 2 diabetes, primarily an insatiable thirst.

I started on Glucophage, because there was no generic metformin back then. I took 850 mg dosage 3 x a day, but I had stomach problems. My doctor put me on a lower dose, 500 3x, and that was fine. Three months later, he wanted me to try 850 mg again. I said I had a real bad time with it. He said he knew that, but that by now my body would have adjusted to it and I likely would have no problems. Darned if he wasn't right!

My A1c bounced around the 7's, if it got too high we added another medication. I stuck to the diet fairly well, but in my 40's I did not get enough exercise. I had a bad shoulder, dislocated frequently in my 20's, then had what is called Bristow surgery when I was 30. That stopped the dislocation, but limited mobility in my right shoulder (I am right handed). No softball, volleyball, or throwing a football. I always enjoyed them when younger, I've always wondered how much, if any, the injury contributed to diabetes. I like games, but I don't like to exercise per se.

I was on glipizide for a number of years. It lowered my glucose, often too much. I had lows in the low 40's, 2 or 3 times a week. I was on several medications by that time, I really did not know much about the them, I just did what I was told by my doctor and counted carbohydrates.

At age 54 I moved to a small town in South Dakota. My A1c improved dramatically from exercise. In 2004 my A1c's were 6.0, 6.4, 5.6, and 6.2 Looking back, a 5.6 on pills after 10 years of type 2 was remarkable. It was just the situation I was in, a byproduct of a more active lifestyle. I thought I had this diabetes thing figured out!

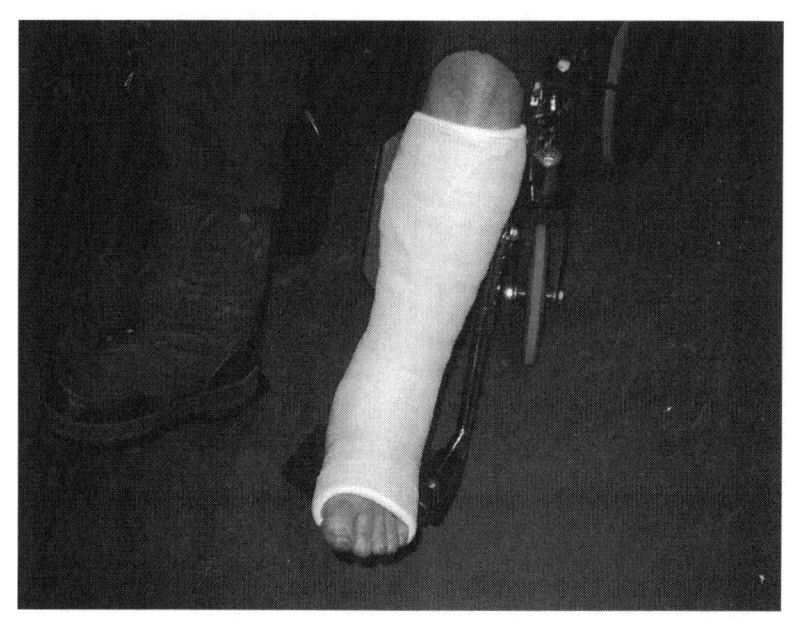

In 2005 my A1c's were 7.4, 6.9, and 8.4 What's with the 8.4? I drove home 200 miles in the freezing rain, the Sunday after Thanksgiving. My ATV was outdoors, and I was going to put it in the shed. I pulled up to the shed, then swung my leg over to get off (like you do on a motorcycle or bicycle), and my foot slipped off the footrest down to the ground, dislocated, and broke both bones in my lower leg.

I had my cell phone in my pocket, and called for help. I needed help badly. The power was off in our town for about 5 days from the freezing rain, and it was a week before the surgeon could operate on my leg. I spent 3 months in a wheelchair, and then crutches, and finally a cane. Before long the leg felt OK, it did heal well, except tendons were too short so the range of motion is a bit limited. I can't lift my left toe up as high as the right, with my heels on the floor. While in the wheelchair, I went online to diabetes forums, to find what exercises I could do.

At this time my A1c jumped from 7.1 to 8.7, in three months, with no change at all in medications or life style other than the wheel chair. I really don't like needles, and dragged my feet as far as going on insulin. My doctor let me try adding more medications at mealtime, Precose and Starlix, they only helped a little. So, after 5 months of this with little improvement, I told my doctor "This isn't working" and went on basal insulin. I was expected to need about 30 units per day, my Certified Diabetes Educator (CDE) had me start at 20 units and gradually work my way up, a process called titrating the dose. This way is the safe way, you will find out how much you need without going beyond what you need. I was taking 2 injections, morning and bedtime, and splitting the dosage. It was all new, I was eager to see the results! I kept increasing the dosage every few days, and doing more testing, looking for changes. NONE. Day after day became week after week. As time went by, the injections began to burn. The evening injection was twice as large as the morning one, because my afternoon and evening numbers were considerably better than my morning numbers. It was suggested that I split the evening injection in two, and sure enough two small ones did not sting as much as one large one. Gradually, something like 6 long weeks into the process, my afternoon numbers started to come down a little. The change was enough to notice, but still not sufficient. I kept going up in my dosage until I reached 100 units per day, more than 3 times what was expected. At this point, late afternoon and evening numbers were usually in the 140s. That is better than they were previously, but still unacceptable. I needed more insulin, but it burned so bad I was reluctant to take it. That is just the way lantus is, at high doses.

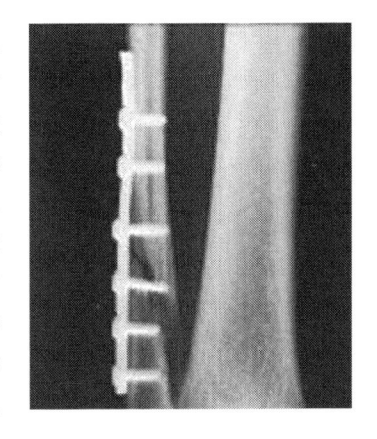

My A1c was down to 7.8, which was much better than the 8.9 I had started with, but if I was going to take insulin, shouldn't I be able to do much better? A call to my doctor resulted in a switch to 70/30 (NPH/Novolog). That is a mixture of rapid acting Novolog and a medium duration NPH. The instructions were to take it with breakfast and supper. I asked, and no, I did not have to start over with the titration, I was to take 100 units per day. The results were better, and it did not sting! When I had my next A1c done, it was 6.9! That part was much improved, and was acceptable, but my fasting numbers were still in the 200 to 250 range. When I started on insulin, I told my CDE that I wanted an insulin pump. I had begun reading about them online. I was told that I needed to do injections first, because that is what you would do in case of pump failure. At this point, I was back to seeing my doctor rather than CDE. I showed him all my graphs and charts of my glucose readings, and told him I wanted a pump, and which one. He said I should do very well on a pump.

I had contacted 3 pump companies, so I had the literature and forms for my choice, which was the Deltec Cozmo. That pump seemed to have many more features that a type 2 would use, including a large cartridge that would hold 300 units of insulin. That is important, if I was going to use more than 100 units a day to get my glucose down where it belonged, I did not want to have to be refilling it often. The Cozmo also had many reminders I could set to remind me to take my pills 3 x a day, and remind me to test 2 hours after taking a bolus, and something called a disconnect bolus to help remind me to hook back up after I disconnected for a shower. I brought the paperwork to my doctor, he seemed a little surprised with my choice, but I explained my reasoning and he could see I had done my homework. In the place on the form where they had checkboxes for Type 1 and Type 2, on the paperwork, he checked neither. He wrote, "Insulin dependent." This was very true, just not exactly the question they asked. It worked, and I think it is a very clever way to do the paperwork. By this time it was quite apparent I had Dawn Phenomenon, so this also went on the paperwork. Next came the waiting for insurance approval. I had heard online that this can sometimes take quite a while, I had prepared myself for several weeks wait. Three days later I got a phone call with the news that I had been approved, and apologizing for how long it had taken! It seems the person who was to make the decision was out of the office. I was told I would receive a phone call from a pump trainer to schedule an appointment. That took a day or two, I ended up with an appointment about a week after the news that I was approved.

I had a mid morning appointment, and another in the afternoon. I had read the manual for the pump online, working the pump was not going to be a problem. The manuals are available for download in PDF form, from the pump manufacturers. Reading that can be a help in deciding which pump you want. If you can enter names and numbers into a phone list on a cell phone, you can work a pump. Most pumps have some kind of trial or demo period. I live a long way from a metropolitan area, or likely I would have been able to have a sales representative show me the pump, at least.

I was somewhat nervous about installing the infusion set, and about whether I would remember everything I needed to know the next day. The pump trainer did all the settings, we talked about all of them so I understood where to set them and what they did. The trainer was a very good Nurse Practitioner CDE/Pump Trainer. I learned that I would not be needing 100 units a day, because the rapid acting Apidra insulin in the pump is much more efficient than the Lantus was. The trainer had a 200 mile drive to return home, so there was no luxury of a dry run with a saline solution. We started right in with the Apidra. I went out for lunch, took my insulin, and returned to the office for further instruction. I asked questions, she answered, and vice versa. She set up several basal rates, with a lot more basal insulin to be delivered at night. My first night on a pump, I was a little apprehensive. I set an alarm to wake myself up at 3 am, because you don't want to go too low in the middle of the night.

One hundred seven the next morning! I had hoped to get my fasting readings of 200 to 250 down by 40 points at least. I never in my wildest dreams expected more than a 100 point drop. The trainer called back a few hours later, she was about to leave for home. When I told her about the 107, she sounded quite pleased and more than a little surprised. She asked questions about how I would do adjustments, and what to do if this or that happened. Then she said that I was not a beginner, but an advanced intermediate. I guess studying the manual had paid off!

I started off with a TDD (Total Daily Dose) of 55 units of Apidra. I spent considerable time making small changes in my basal rates, insulin carbohydrate ratios, and correction factor. All these are to get the pump to give you the right amount of insulin at the right time. When I started out my standard deviation was about 25. Thats not too bad, but within the first year I got that down to 14.

This means my readings were increasingly closer to my average. Another way of saying that is I had fewer lows and highs, as I got better at making adjustments.

My first A1c on the pump was 5.7%. That's a good number, but not as good as I expected. Many of the charts I had seen that match average glucose to expected A1c are just way off. They'd have you believe an average of 100 would get you an A1c of 5. It doesn't work that way, at least not for me. Just after my first A1c, my insurance changed prescription management companies, and I could no longer get Apidra. I had to switch to Novolog or Humalog, I chose Novolog. I had to increase my insulin to keep the same numbers. When all was said and done, my insulin had gone up 24% in about 2 weeks. After the first A1c of 5.7%, my A1c continued to fall. 5.5%, 5.3%, 4.9% Wow! I had two 4.9's in a row, doing that without serious lows is really hard work. No room for any mistakes at all! I eased up a little, but at this point I have had 16 in a row of 5.4 or lower, and my current A1c is 5.0%.

During this time, from the start of insulin on, I became increasingly involved in the online community, learning, helping, teaching, and writing. I was moderator on a couple of online forums. Then I got burned out, dealing with people who were there for reasons other than mutual diabetes support, so I left for over a year before returning. If others can learn from my mistakes and my success, that would be a very good thing.

My 15 Minutes of Fame

In the fall of 2008, I saw a post on one of the forums I frequent "I'm looking for diabetes success stories." No indication what for, and the name of the person that left the post meant nothing to me. I considered myself a success story, I had many A1c's in the low 5's, lipids, and Blood Pressure under control, and I'd lost more than 30 pounds. I took a chance and sent a private message in reply. I got an email from Tracey Neithercott at Diabetes

Forecast, the magazine of the American Diabetes Association. We set up a time for a telephone interview.

The interview lasted 45 minutes, she asked many questions, and gave me time to tell my story. I had some reservations about giving my full name, online it is pseudonyms or first names, but if no name, no story, so I went ahead. I've never regretted it. The article is in the December '08 issue of Diabetes Forecast It really came out well, and all the important information is correct. I was surprised and pleased to see that my advocacy and practice of fairly low carbohydrate eating is in the article. The ADA has historically not advocated low carbohydrate eating.

I live in a rural area, and tried to start a support group in the local small town. I did a feature interview with the county weekly newspaper, we talked about the magazine article, and I talked about diabetes and my wish to start a support group. I left contact information in the article, but it generated no phone calls, sad to say. I did hear from a few diabetics that saw the article, months later, and "confessed" they were diabetics, but did not want anyone to know. I don't understand that attitude, though I suspect it is mixed in with "it's my own fault" guilt. For more on this see the chapter on "frequent problems."

Just Diagnosed?

You have just been diagnosed with Type 2 diabetes. What now?

- Educate yourself about diabetes, about what is happening and what you can do about it.
- Go to a diabetes education class, read a book, ask your doctor for information, find a diabetes support group, whatever works for you.
- Check out an online forum and ask questions. Most of us were too shocked to think of questions for our Doctor when first diagnosed.
- Get a food scale, and learn to count carbohydrates. Why carbohydrates? We'll cover that in a later chapter. There are quite a few food scales that can be found online. Look for one that can be zeroed (tare function).
- Find something that you like to do, that will give you some physical exercise. Half an hour of walking each day is sufficient, but most any exercise is good.
- Get a glucose meter, record your readings and what time they were taken.

Diabetes Management

Successful management of type 1

Success can depend on these:

- Skill at counting carbohydrates
- Record keeping, so you don't repeat your mistakes
- Developing good habits

If you are having trouble with the accuracy of your bolus, try reducing your carbohydrate intake. This is certainly not necessary for all type 1s, but it can be a big help if you are experiencing roller coaster glucose readings. Smaller amounts of carbohydrates mean smaller errors in carbohydrate estimation and smaller errors in bolus.

Successful management of type 2

My intent here is to pass on what I think are most important tools for successful management of Type 2, that is what I have and what I know most about. Much of it will also apply to other types of diabetes.

The 3 stages of Type 2

Calling these stages is my idea and outlook, but the divisions themselves are standard medical procedure.

The result, for all types of diabetes, is the higher your glucose is above normal, and the longer it is high, the greater the chance of diabetes complications. High variability can also be a factor leading to complications.

Stage 1, Pre-diabetes

Two fasting readings of 100 (5.55 in the UK system) or greater, but less than 126 (7) puts you in this category. An A1c of 5.7 to 6.4 will also put you in this category. Pre-diabetes is characterized by having insulin resistance, and reduced capacity of your pancreas to produce insulin. What is insulin resistance? It means your body cannot use insulin efficiently and that you need more of it to get the same job done.

What does insulin do? It is a hormone that allows your body to get glucose (sugar) out of your blood, and into the cells of your body where it is used for energy.

We only have one pancreas, it has cells in it that are called beta cells, their job is to produce insulin. We are all normally born with the capacity to produce more insulin than our body needs. For the sake of example, lets say a pancreas can produce 3 times what you will need. By the time you are diagnosed as pre-diabetic, your pancreas can only produce about half as much as it used to be able to. So now you can make one and a half times as much as a non-diabetic would need. That sounds like you would still be OK, but the problem is that due to insulin resistance, you can't use the insulin efficiently. Lets say for example, you now need twice as much insulin as you once did. So, in summary, you need twice as much as a person without insulin resistance, but you only make one and a half times as much as a person without resistance and a normal pancreas would need, so you have a relative shortage of insulin.

Without enough insulin, the level of glucose in your blood rises. It is this rise in glucose that is spotted by blood tests, and waves a red flag at medical personnel that this person has some kind of insulin problem, likely diabetes.

I personally think pre-diabetes is not a good name, what you have is mild diabetes. If you think of it that way, you really get a better picture of what is going on.

At this stage you have the opportunity of a lifetime. You can slow down or stop entirely the progression of diabetes. How does Type 2 diabetes progress? Primarily, by the capacity of your beta cells to produce insulin being decreased as time goes on, but also your insulin resistance tends to increase.

So...what can you do to help yourself?

1) If you have excess weight, lose it. This is one of the hardest things to do, but the most worthwhile, for many reasons. Remember, this is not all or nothing. A 10% weight loss will make a significant change in your health, and a reduction in insulin resistance. Being overweight increases insulin resistance.

2) The more you weigh, the more you eat to support that weight, which means the more insulin you need. Exercising at least half an hour 5 times a week will lower your insulin resistance. It will also assist in loosing weight, if that is needed.

3) Reduce your carbohydrate intake. Carbohydrates, which are sugars and starches, are what gets turned into glucose in your bloodstream. To the extent you limit your carbohydrates, you are limiting how much rise in your glucose will happen after eating. Also, limiting your carbohydrates almost invariably limits your calorie intake also. This helps you loose weight, if you need to do that. We'll talk more about this in a later chapter.

The main characteristics that are evident at this stage is the ability to treat the problem successfully without the help of medicine, and the ability to slow down, stop, and sometimes reverse the progression of diabetes.

Stage 2, Type 2 Diabetes.

Fasting glucose greater than 126 (7)

Things are more serious here, in that it is not reversible at this stage, and it is not clear that any method exists to slow the progression. There is a school of thought though, that high glucose speeds up the loss of beta cells.

The thing to remember is high glucose causes the complications, not diabetes itself. How successfully you and your medical team treat your diabetes, will directly affect your chances of complications.

What to do:
- Lose any excess weight, diet, and exercise
- Oral medications (pills)

Most often the first medication given is metformin (trade name Glucophage). It acts by reducing glucose release by your liver and helping reduce your insulin resistance. It is a very safe medicine, does not cause you to go low, and has been in use for decades. It is very common to get gastrointestinal upset in the first week or two you take it, but that usually goes away. Metformin is considered weight neutral, some people have reported losing a little weight when taking metformin. If gastrointestinal problems persist with metformin, try the extended release version, that often helps.

Other medications reduce your insulin resistance, cause you to digest food more slowly, and cause your pancreas to produce all the insulin it can. We'll look at them in a later chapter.

Stage 3, Insulin dependent type 2

As the years go on, what usually happens is your pancreas produces less insulin. Oral medications still function as they did, but the help they provide is no longer sufficient to bridge the gap between the amount of insulin your body produces, and the amount you need.

Often a basal insulin (usually Lantus or Levemir) is prescribed. For about half the type 2 diabetics that try this, it provides enough help. It lowers your glucose some, all the time. If that is not sufficient, or becomes insufficient, then a bolus insulin (usually Novolog, Humalog or Apidra) is added at mealtimes, or a mixture like 70/30 (novolog/NPH) is taken. The mix has the advantage of being taken only twice a day. For those who resist the idea of needles, it can be easier to accept. It has the disadvantage that your mealtimes must be regular and of equal, or nearly so, in carbohydrate content. The lack of flexibility is the primary downside to mixes. Taking basal and bolus insulin separately is more work, but is a much more flexible system, allowing you to adjust your insulin to your food, rather than the other way around. This is also known as MDI (Multiple Daily Injections). MDI usually will produce the best results, if you know what you are doing, short of an insulin pump.

An insulin pump has many advantages, providing maximum flexibility, and allowing you to adjust your basal rates for different activities, and allowing different rates at different times of day. This is very important for those with Dawn Phenomenon, who need to have much higher basal rates during the night than at other times. An insulin pump is also more accurate at delivering basal than MDI.

What to do:
- Lose any excess weight, diet, and exercise
- Metformin and Insulin

Usually an insulin dependent type 2 will continue to take Metformin when they begin to take insulin. This is because it reduces the amount of insulin you need. In my case, it means I need less than half as much as I would without it. Often any additional oral medications you have been taking, are no longer needed. See your doctor about that.

Tools for Success

The Minneapolis Diabetes Expo, by the American Diabetes Association

Knowledge

Learn all you can, from many sources. Treat it like a hobby. What? Yes, like you were just starting to learn about something of interest. You may not like diabetes, few people do, but it needs to be something of interest. If you have no interest in managing your diabetes, neither will your doctor, your family, or anyone else. If not you, then who? Keep at it, it takes years to master. If you join an online community, you can ask questions of more experienced diabetics, and in time, you end up answering questions from people less experienced than yourself. This also keeps you up to date with new methods, new equipment, and new medications that come out from time to time.

Good habits

Test frequently, avoid high carbohydrate foods, don't buy groceries when you are hungry. Allow yourself the occasional treat, just don't go hog wild. A bad day is a bad day, don't let it become a bad week. How often should you test? That depends on your situation, and method of treatment. As a rule, I think you should be testing as often as you need to gain information that you will act on. There is no point in testing 10 times a day, if you don't make use of the information to change your eating habits, medication, or lifestyle. It is in your best interest to get information, and use it to better your diabetes management skills.

Effort

Making sure you have the food on hand that is good for a diabetic, is work. The only way to keep from eating stuff that is not good for you, is to have a choice. For most of us, getting the exercise we need is work. The lucky few who are already doing that, just need to be regular about it. Testing your glucose and recording the results is work. Analyzing the data to see how you might improve your control is also work. It is very much worth the effort, to avoid all the terrible complications that would be more likely to happen if you don't put forth the effort. Another thing to think about, is you will feel better when you are more physically fit.

Assistance From Others

Your Professional Team

- General practitioner
- An Endocrinologist is a medical doctor who specializes in hormones, and the endocrine glands that secrete them. This would include the pituitary, thyroid, adrenals, ovaries, testes and the pancreas.
- CDE (Certified Diabetes Educator) is a clinical psychologist, registered nurse, occupational therapist, optometrist, pharmacist, physical therapist, physician (MD or OD), podiatrist, dietitian, physician assistant, clinical exercise physiologist, or social worker with at least a masters degree, who has a minimum of 1000 hours of specialized training and 2 years experience in their field.
- Diabetes Nurse Practitioner (NP) is a registered nurse who has advanced training and clinical experience, and a minimum of 500 supervised hours. Nurse practitioners differ from CDE in that they can legally prescribe and adjust medications.
- Podiatrist is a Doctor of Podiatric Medicine who specializes in feet, ankles, and related structures of the leg.
- An Ophthalmologist is a medical doctor who specializes in medical and surgical eye problems, and has completed 4 years of residency training after medical school.

A CDE would likely teach you about diabetes when you are first diagnosed, along with a dietitian. An NP or an MD would likely help you manage your diabetes and you would likely have quarterly or semiannual visits. Endocrinologists are scarce, you would be much more likely to have an appointment with one if you are taking insulin, as that can be a much more complex situation. Visits might only be annually, unless there are problems that your MD or NP needs assistance with. These are generalizations that do not always hold, but there are only about 4,000 Endocrinologists in the USA.

INTERNET RESOURCES

Forums

These are online communities of diabetics, families of diabetics, and caregivers who provide mutual support and knowledge about diabetes. Some have tens of thousands of members. It gives you a place to ask questions, get opinions, and sometimes just to have someone to listen to your problems, who has been there. Some of the ones I have found very helpful are Diabetes Daily.com, DiabetesForums.com, and Tu-Diabetes.org. There are also forums on Facebook and Yahoo. You can start out reading, and when you want to post a question or make an observation, you join the forum, and choose a name for yourself. Members don't have access to your personal information such as physical address or email address, just what you choose to share (like the city you live in, what type of diabetes you have, and maybe your age). I have developed many long term friendships online with people in other parts of the United States and all over the world. When you post a message, it is like leaving a note on a bulletin board at a grocery store, everyone can read it. You can also send private messages to people, if they have selected to allow that option. Some forums have chat areas, where several people can chat (text) in real time. That is more immediate, it's all a matter of personal taste and what you are looking for.

Newsreaders

I use google reader. It uses the google search engine to look for topics I select, diabetes is one of them. It finds all kinds of professional articles, product announcements and medical studies relating to diabetes.

Online Buying

I live in a rural area, and the stores do not carry some items for diabetics. I buy things like almond flour (low carbohydrate) online.

Trial and Error

I often joke with my diabetic friends, that diabetes should be renamed "Trial and Error." So many things are just try it out and see.

The first medication of choice for a type 2 is Metformin. Most people have some gastronomical upset from it, though some don't. Most people's bodies adjust to it in a week or two, some people never can adjust, they need to switch to another medication. Some can handle lower doses, but not high doses.

When it is time for a T2 to start on insulin, usually a basal insulin is tried first, and for about half the people who try it, that is enough. There is no way to tell if this will work, other than trying it out. They start you out on a low dose, less than the best guess on how much you will need. Then, the dosage is gradually raised, until your numbers start to fall in line. Even then, the post meal tests may show that you also need bolus insulin. If you do, go through the same adjustments to see how much insulin you need for a given amount of carbohydrates, this is known as your insulin-carbohydrate ratio.

When you count carbohydrates, you know how much bolus insulin to take. Some people find that they can subtract fiber from the total, for others that does not work. I count carbohydrates only, some people need to account for protein also.

Beyetta is an injectable that some people take to manage their type 2. Some people get nausea from taking it, some don't. Some people lose weight when taking it, some don't.

Different foods affect people in unexpected ways. Sometimes you get a much bigger rise than the amount of carbohydrates listed on the packaging would lead you to expect. I need to take about one and one half times as much insulin for rice, as the carbohydrates on the label would lead me to expect. This is too many for my carbohydrate budget, so I seldom have rice (even brown rice). I can eat salted in the shell peanuts all day, and get a paltry 5 point rise in my glucose. Most foods fall in line for me, my bolus works out well, but there are these few exceptions, and trial and error is the only way to find what they may be.

When you are sick, insulin requirements may change. Some people require more insulin, some less.

Attitude is Paramount

Have confidence in yourself and your ability to do what needs doing.

1. If your attitude is "I am going to do whatever it takes to have success at managing my diabetes," then barring other medical conditions or circumstances beyond your control you are almost guaranteed success.
2. If your attitude is "I'm going to try it and see how it goes," you have a chance at succeeding.
3. If your attitude is "I just have a little sugar problem," "I'm too busy to do all that stuff" and so forth, then you can expect to fail. The less you do to take care of your problem, the worse it gets and the faster it gets bad.

Overcoming Fear

Most of us have a fear of the unknown. Also, we have heard of all the bad things that happen to some diabetics. I have found through my own experience, that the best way to curb fear and worry is to learn all you can about diabetes, and to do all you can to keep your glucose in line. Once you begin to see things getting better, it helps inspire you. Being in a group situation, whether online or in person, helps a lot with the feeling that you are alone. It provides companionship, and people who understand what you are experiencing.

A good doctor can be a big help, one you trust and one that trusts you. You always have to remember though, that unlike many medical conditions, the majority of the treatment for diabetes is up to you. Medicine alone will never do the job. You need to take control of your food intake and exercise.

Keeping your own records can help you to see how things are progressing, this is especially vital if you are taking insulin. I turned my condition around, you can too!

Take Ownership of your Diabetes

What do I mean by that? It is your diabetes. It is your problem to solve. It is your task to learn as much as you can. It is your responsibility to figure out what to eat, and an exercise program that works for you. You have to find a doctor, endocrinologist, NP or CDE that will work with you. In short, it is your life! Professionals can help with ideas and specialized knowledge, but ask yourself this "What percentage of the time are they around to help me?" Perhaps 15 minutes every 3 months? The more you take on yourself, the more successful you will be at avoiding complications. If you are on insulin, you need to understand insulin and carbohydrates and make adjustments as needed. Having your doctor make the adjustments just does not work well, the process is too slow. Diabetes is all about trial and error. You make an adjustment, then test. You need to try the adjustment out for a few days, to see if it is an improvement. If it is better, have you reached your desired results yet? Is it time for another adjustment? A doctor just does not have time for this.

If you are on oral medications, what you eat is a big part of your results. If you eat more carbohydrates than your body can handle, high glucose will result, every time. How many carbohydrates can your body handle? Use your meter and your brain to figure it out! Hint: Trial and error again.

Remember, diabetes is a marathon, not a sprint. You can't learn it all at once. Just make a start. Some things will work for you if you accept them, and later it will hit you in an "aha" moment, "so that's why that worked!" Notice which medicines work, leave why they work for later.

I strongly suggest that you teach yourself to be really good at counting carbohydrates. It is needed for all kinds of diabetes. The reason is simple, carbohydrates are what raises your glucose the most, by far.

Frequent Problems

Denial

Denial happens quite often. "There has to be some mistake, I feel great!", you say, when your doctor tells you that you have diabetes. "You said pre-diabetes? Thats not so bad then, nothing to worry about." "I just have a little sugar problem." On and on goes the list. The crux of the problem is patients who duck the problem, rather than facing it. It is hard for some to face, with unknowns, and the fact that it is for the rest of your life. That's a tough one at first. Usually, after while, the diabetic does an about face and decides to do something about it. The sad part is, during the time of denial damage may be done to your body that can't be fixed.

The most important thing I can say to someone in denial, is that it does not get better on it's own, it only gets worse. With knowledge and effort by the diabetic, and help from a medical professional, it will get better instead of worse.

Guilt

"It's my own fault." I hear this almost every day. Let's take a look at that statement. What is the first thing that a newly diagnosed diabetic goes through? Diabetes education. Why? Very few people know much about diabetes, unless they have had it a while, or a loved one has it. We all know that if you eat too much you are likely to gain weight. It's true that can be an element in type 2, but most overweight people do not get diabetes. Genetics is part of it, and there is mounting evidence that it is, in part, an autoimmune problem like type 1. Guilt is not justified, and is very counter productive. All that energy being spent feeling sorry for yourself, needs to be directed at making your situation better. Diabetes is not a death sentence, unless you make it so.

I work hard at diabetes management, it is expensive, consumes my time, requires sacrifice and it is inconvenient. It is something to be taken seriously, but not something to be feared. I don't worry about it, the health risks are minimal if you keep your glucose in good control. Like most people, I knew next to nothing about it before I was diagnosed.

Depression

Diabetes increases your chance of depression. The connection seems to be the stress of managing your diabetes, the fact that it does not end, and diabetes complications. Also if your diabetes is under poor control, symptoms can sometimes look like depression, without being so. When you are depressed, you are less likely to take good care of your diabetes, which in turn makes the diabetes worse.

Most people with diabetes do not suffer depression, but please seek professional help if you do. This is one more reason that working hard to be successful in managing your diabetes is worthwhile.

Know Thyself

To have success in gaining the upper hand in managing diabetes, you have to learn to be honest with yourself about your strengths and weaknesses. The trick is to aim for good habits, and allow yourself the exceptions. I'll give you a few examples. The first one is simple, plan things so that you go grocery shopping after you have eaten. So many things are tempting impulse buys, it's much easier to avoid them if you are not hungry. Also, shop with a list, and stick to it. If they are giving out samples at the grocery store, I might have a cookie or other treat, but I know if I buy a bag or box of whatever, I'll end up eating it in far too little time. For me, it is much easier to not buy it at all, and avoid the temptation at home. For some people this isn't a problem.

Managing diabetes is a marathon, not a sprint. You have to find methods that work for you, that you can sustain over the long haul. Forcing yourself to do things you don't like to do, is not likely to work out well, except in the short run. I have found that avoiding foods that I like, but that do not work out for me due to too many carbohydrates, is not that hard to do. I still let myself have a treat occasionally. I don't force myself to eat anything that I don't like though.

Make sure that there are plenty of foods available you do like, and that work for you. I think for most of us, going hungry is not the way to success. Who can stick with something that results in your being hungry all the time for the rest of your life?

Diet and Exercise

Carbohydrates make your clothes shrink

Carbohydrates are primarily what raises your glucose. To the extent you limit your carbohydrates, you are limiting how much of a rise in your glucose will happen after eating. Also, limiting your carbohydrates almost invariably limits your calorie intake. This helps you loose weight, if that is your goal. In my case, I found that 80 grams of carbohydrate a day works for me. I have lost weight, kept it off for more than 3 years at this point, and it has helped with my glucose control. You will need to find how much carbohydrate works for you. Your scale and glucose meter can help you decide.

Carbohydrate counting is important for all types of diabetes. Some people can control their Type 2 diabetes with diet and exercise. Does that just mean eat good foods? Well, that is a part of it, but all carbohydrates raise your blood sugar, not just sugar. Just because a food doesn't taste sweet, doesn't mean it won't raise your blood glucose. Fruit from tropical climates has more sugar in it than fruit from temperate climates. Bananas, oranges and pineapple require a lot more insulin (natural or injected) than berries.

Exercise will usually lower glucose. If you are controlling your diabetes with diet and exercise, limiting your amount of carbohydrate intake can help control spikes in your blood glucose, and therefore help you reduce your risk of complications such as heart disease, amputation, and eye problems.

Many people with type 2 diabetes are on oral medications to help them control their blood sugar. They work by different mechanisms. Some will prevent your liver from releasing too much glycogen (stored glucose), while others will increase insulin sensitivity, while still others will push your pancreas to release more insulin. Some medications work by multiple means. While these drugs can be a big help, most of them have as a side effect, weight gain. Weight gain for most people is a natural effect of controlling blood sugar. You stop spilling glucose in your urine, and stop turning excess glucose into triglycerides. Added body weight usually leads to added insulin resistance, which raises blood sugar and you end up with still more fat stored-a vicious circle. This makes limiting carbohydrate intake even more important. It helps break the cycle. A natural progression of type 2 is the pancreas beta cells "exhausting." The pancreas can no longer keep up with the high insulin needs, and needs help. The help comes as injected insulin. There are many different forms of injected insulin, and all type 1s, most type 1.5s, and some type 2s and gestational diabetics need it in some way. Any way you do it, however, this basic idea needs to remain in your mind. Insulin and exercise lower blood sugar, while carbohydrates raise it. Therefore, you want these things to balance to prevent your glucose from going too high or too low.

If you are on an insulin pump, you use buttons on the pump to tell the pump how many carbohydrates you are going to eat, most pumps will do the math to give you the right amount of insulin to match the carbohydrates, once they have been properly adjusted.

You can also use "Multiple Daily Injections" to match your insulin dose to what you eat. With MDI you take an injection of long acting insulin once or twice a day, and then take injections of fast acting insulin every time you eat (unless, of course, you are eating because you are low).

Diabetes is a progressive disease. Type 1's leave the "honeymoon phase" while type 2s deal with increased insulin resistance and more beta cell exhaustion. Type 1.5s also are on a path where less and less insulin is produced. The further you are along this path, the harder glucose control becomes, and the more careful you need to be with your carbohydrate counting. Counting carbohydrates is part science and part art. You can read labels and check in books when at home and measure and weigh foods. When you eat out, you have to guesstimate. That takes practice, the more you do it the better you get, just like most things in life.

How to Count Carbohydrates:

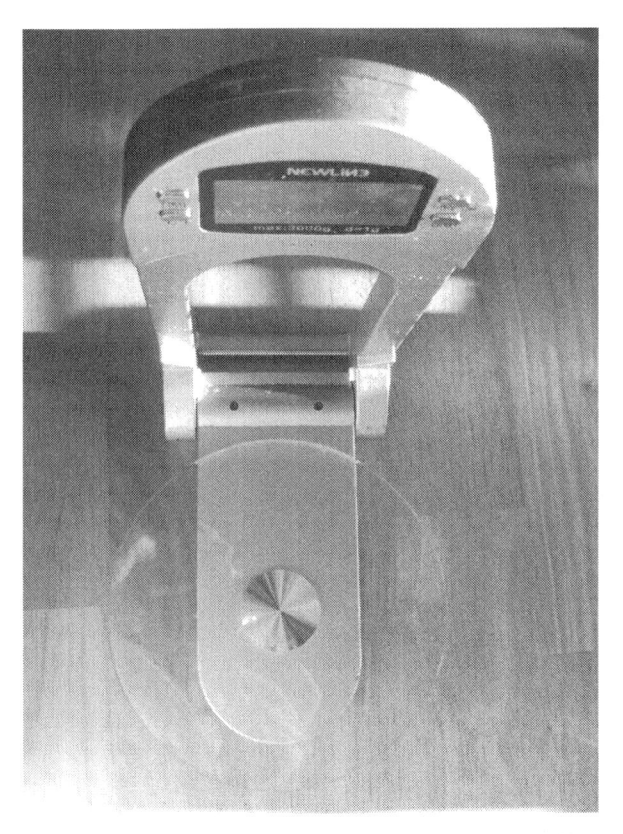

Food scales.

A food scale is small, fairly inexpensive, and the most accurate way we know to measure portion sizes. In the US, we would look for one that reads in both ounces and grams, and what is called a Tare button. That simply means it has a button to set the scale to zero whenever you wish. I like the style in the photo, because you can put most containers on it and still be able to read the scale, with the readings on the bottom front that can be more difficult.

Here is a good way to use the scale:

- Put a plate on the scale.
- Set the scale to zero.
- Add food to the plate, until the desired amount shows on the scale.
- Set the scale to zero
- Add another food.

You end up with a plate with food on it, and you now know how much of each food you have. This way you have not dirtied any measuring cups doing it. The package, can, box, or book you are looking in will tell you how many carbohydrates in a serving. You can weigh out two-thirds of a serving, for instance, and you will have two-thirds of the carbohydrates.

If a food is only listed in a volume measure like a cup of milk, you can do this:

- Put a measuring cup on the scale
- Zero the scale
- Add a cup of milk
- Write down how many grams a cup of milk weighs.

From here on, you can put a glass on the scale, zero it, and add a cup of milk without measuring, just add the right weight.

Some scales have even more helpful features. Some scales have food databases right in them, or let you enter the carbohydrates per serving and figure the exact carbohydrate for you, not just the weight. Some scales will even total it for you as you go along.

There are many, many ways to figure out how many carbohydrates are in foods. The Cozmo, some Animas, and Omnipod insulin pumps have food databases right in them, while Accu-Chek and Calorie King make software programs that can be loaded onto a PDA with a carbohydrate database.

There are also many web sites, with Calorie King being a popular and thorough one.

Medications

ORAL MEDICATIONS (PILLS)
Metformin

Metformin is usually the first medication given to a type 2. It is very safe, and very effective. Usually, it takes a while for your body to get used to it. The first week can be a huge problem for some, with gastrointestinal upset and sometimes diarrhea. This is usually less of a problem by the second week. Usually, a persons body adjusts to it, and has no symptoms at all by the third week or so. For some, symptoms don't recede, and they end up needing to switch to a different medication. Why is it worth it to give metformin a serious try? Most type 2 medications have weight gain as a side effect. Metformin is weight neutral. It was designed as a weight loss drug, it just never worked out for that purpose. There are generics, so that helps keep the cost down. Metformin helps with insulin resistance, but primarily it keeps your liver from releasing too much glucose. So, it helps prevent highs without causing low glucose. It also has some benefit in protecting your heart. It comes in 1000, 850 and 500 mg doses, and an extended release version which is easier on the stomach. The extended release version is not available as generic so it is more expensive. I've been taking metformin for around 17 years, it gives me no problems at all now. It did at first, so I stepped down from the 850 mg dosage to the 500 mg and all was well. About 3 months later, I went back to the 850 s and had no problem. The usual method is to start with a low dose, and work your way up, as your body adjusts to it. It is one of the most commonly taken medications of any kind. It takes 3 to 5 weeks for metformin to have full effect, as it builds up in your body.

These are just my own thoughts and experiences, please seek the advice of your doctor on this or any medication.

Sulfonylureas

This class of drug act by increasing the release of insulin from the beta cells in the pancreas. They are effective, but can be too effective, causing hypoglycemia. Think of them as turning your pancreas on "full." Glipizide and Glimpride are examples of Sulfonylureas. I used Glipizide for many years, and would have lows in the low 40's several times a week. The problem arrises because you don't have much control over the dosage with a pill, the way you can with an injectable like insulin. For some, it can work fine, but use caution.

These are just my own thoughts and experiences, please seek the advice of your doctor on this or any medication.

Thiazolidinediones

These drugs help with insulin sensitivity.

Avandia (no longer available) and Actos are members of this class. Typical improvement of A1c is about one and one half to two percent The downside to Actos is weight gain. I was on it about 10 years, and lost 7 pounds the month I stopped taking it. I had no other problems with it other than the weight gain.

Alpha-glucosidase Inhibitors

These drugs slow down your digestion. Precose and Glyset are examples of these. They don't help a whole lot, about one half to one percent on your A1c. I took precose for a few months, I noticed the difference but it did not help me enough to be the solution for me.

Peptide analogs

Byetta and Victoza are examples of this class. Two problems, these are often not covered by insurance, and Byetta can cause nausea, which usually passes in a few weeks as your body adjusts.

Meglitinides
These are taken with meals to help with the insulin response to the meal. Prandin and Starlix are examples. I took Starlix and got very little help from it.

PEPTIDE ANALOGS (INJECTABLES)
Examples are Galvus, Januvia, and Onglyza. Typically they help one half to one percent on your A1c.

Linagliptin, a DPP4 inhibitor was just approved in pill form. Expect a .7 percent drop in A1c

INSULIN

Rapid acting
This starts acting in 5 to 15 minutes, and lasts for 3 to 4 hours. You take these slightly before, during, or slightly after a meal. You vary the amount of insulin proportional to the amount of carbohydrates you are eating. Common examples: Humalog, Novolog, and Apidra

Short Acting
Starts working within 30 minutes and is active for about 5 to 8 hours. It is relatively inexpensive, but for many is not likely to give you results as good as rapid acting. Example: "Regular"

Intermediate Acting
Starts working in 1 to 3 hours and lasts 16 to 24 hours. Example NPH. The big downside to NPH, it has uneven action. There is a big peak that often causes people to go very low, usually about 7 hours after taking it. It is relatively inexpensive. I have heard it called "insulin from hell" by a number of people

who experienced really bad lows. It can, however, work fine in some circumstances for type 2 diabetics, especially if they have Dawn Phenomenon.

Long acting

Examples Lantus and Levemir. They start working in about an hour. Lantus lasts about 24 hours, Levemir is designed to be injected twice daily. Lantus can "burn" when you inject high doses, the fluid that contains Lantus is a little acidic.

Mix

There are insulins that are a mix of rapid acting and intermediate acting. 70/30 (NPH/Novolog) is an example. They are made to be taken twice a day. The trouble with that method is you cannot vary the amount with the amount of carbohydrates you are eating, because it is has both basal and bolus insulin in it. That means, that you match your food carbohydrate content to the insulin, instead of the other way around. Also, the insulin and the food need to be taken at specific times. This is a very restrictive regimen. It is simple, and since it requires only 2 injections, many type 2's elect this option. I really don't recommend it. I was on it for about half a year. My A1c was OK, but due to Dawn Phenomenon, my fasting test results were quite bad, and there is no way to fix that on a mix.

Supplements

I take Vitamin D3, Lovaza and low dose Aspirin.

- Type 2 diabetics are often low on Vitamin D, it showed up on my blood tests that I am.

- I take low dose Aspirin as a heart precaution (it thins your blood).

- Lovaza is concentrated fish oil, to help with lipids.

Glucose Meter

It is a very important tool

It's not a very complex tool, but it is extremely important to a diabetic. The most common questions I am asked is "When should I test?", and "How often should I test?"

If you are on insulin, testing your glucose when you wake up is important. You want to correct any errors that have crept in while sleeping. Testing before breakfast is important if a significant time has gone by since you tested. A type 2 would normally test again 2 hours after eating. What you are testing for, is to see if your meal bolus was the correct amount. If it is not enough, you can do a correction. If it is too much, and you are low, a glucose tab or food would be in order. A type 1 might need to test at 3 or 4 hours, rather than 2 hours, depending on what works for them. The last test would be before bed. If your glucose varies a lot, I would do a test and correction a couple of hours before bed. You really want to be as stable as you can manage at bedtime. In my own case, I have dawn phenomenon, I do a test and a correction by pump just before bed. My glucose is quite stable, and I really have no problems with lows at night.

Another reason to test, is to find how various foods affect you. The peak you get from food will be something like an hour after eating, usually. You can do tests at a half hour and then every 15 minutes until you are on your way back down to your pre meal level, to determine how long it takes for you to peak. Once you know (45 minutes for me), then that is when you will test to find out how various foods affect you. This testing is also valuable for diabetics that are not on insulin. It helps you find what foods work for you, and which you should avoid.

Basal testing. My goal is to set my basal rate so that if I do not eat, my glucose will not drift up or down. That way, if a meal is delayed, or I need to eat early, I won't have any problems. This is easier to do with a pump than injections, but your goal should be the same.

Continuous Glucose Monitor

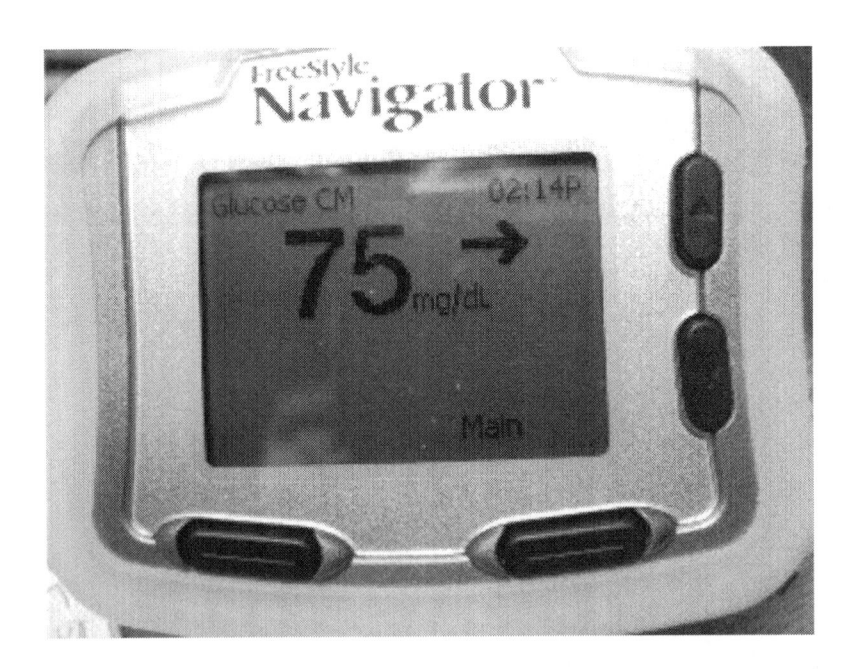

What the heck is that?

A continuous glucose monitor has a sensor that goes under the skin and wirelessly transmits the amount of glucose which is in your interstitial fluid. This is the fluid that is between the cells of your body. The receiver tells you what your glucose reading is, whether it is going up, down, or is relatively stable.

How well does it work?

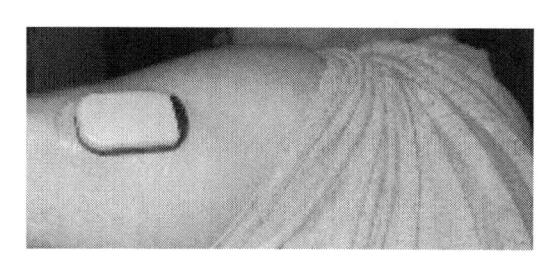

For me, it has worked very well. There is a glucose monitor built in to the receiver that is used to calibrate the system, so it can never be more accurate than the finger sticks used to calibrate it. If you look closely at the graph, the small triangle represents the calibration I did. You can get all kinds of statistics and average, including an important one called standard deviation. Other Continuous monitors calibrate in slightly different manner, but presently all use test strips and fingertip blood samples.

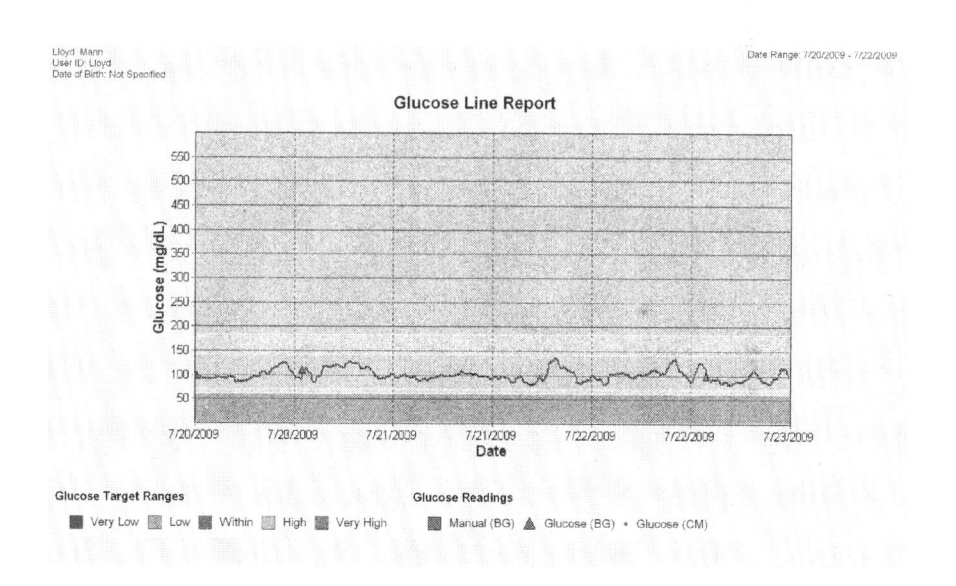

How do you get one?

A continuous glucose monitor system (cgms) requires a doctors prescription. As of this writing, they are not hard to get in the USA, but...some insurance will pay for them, some will not. I have a high deductible, so mine doesn't. I use mine primarily for setting my basal rates on my pump. I have dawn phenomenon, so there are more than a dozen basal rates that need to be set. It is so much better to review the charts in the morning, rather than stay up all night testing every half hour.

A continuous monitor was a great help in learning what kind of adjustments need to be made when you exercise, and are on insulin. I have found that when I go for a five mile walk, I need to eat 25 grams of carbohydrate before I leave, and 35 in the last third of a walk, to keep from going low. The Navigator has a very cool feature, in some situations it can predict a low or a high, a half hour ahead of time, based on where your glucose is right now, and the rate of change you are experiencing. One day, while walking, my glucose was at 104 but the alarm sounded, the navigator predicted a low. I stopped walking, ate some dried fruit, and resumed walking about 15 minutes later. Because I was warned of the low ahead of time, I stopped it at 68!

What is it good for?

If you are unable to feel hypoglycemia, it can warn you ahead of time, and again when you reach limits that you set.

It will warn you if you have high glucose. This can be a huge help if you have a pump occlusion (blockage in the tubing or cannula).

It is a huge help in setting basal rates, especially at night. You can look at graphs of what your glucose was last night, and make adjustments to basal rates. This is especially helpful if you have an insulin pump, where different rates can be set for each half hour, and small adjustments to rates are possible.

Using Insulin

Possible weight gain: insulin is not usually the cause

If your glucose is high, your body does 2 things to try to lower it. Glucose leaves your body in your urine, and excess glucose is turned into triglycerides (a form of fat).

Insulin helps our body get glucose out of our bloodstream in into the cells of our body, where it is used for energy.

Insulin is called a "fat storage hormone," it's true, and that is one of its functions. Note: It is EXCESS GLUCOSE that gets turned into triglycerides. Insulin is not the bad guy when it comes to excess weight, high glucose is!

The way to take care of Type 2 is to do what you need to get your glucose down and keep it down in a more normal range. Exercise lowers glucose. Oral medications reduce your insulin resistance, reduce the glucose your liver releases, slow down the digestion of food (to reduce spikes) or induce your pancreas to create more insulin. I don't recommend the last one, you can have bad lows since there is little control of the dosage, and in my opinion, it causes the burn out the beta cells in your pancreas. Injecting insulin, or infusing insulin with a pump will get your glucose down. One very important tool for controlling your glucose is to reduce your carbohydrate intake. Carbohydrates are by far the largest source of glucose for your body. You need some, but if you get more than you need it is stored as fat. When your glucose is in a normal range, your body stops spilling glucose in your urine, and it stops storing glucose as triglycerides.

Having read this, can you see why high triglycerides are a warning sign of impending diabetes? As we build up fat in our bodies, our insulin resistance goes up (we use insulin less efficiently). At some point, we just don't have enough insulin to make use of the glucose in our blood, so the glucose goes too high - T2 diabetes.

Goals for insulin use

Basal insulin only: When used alone: to lower your glucose somewhat, all the time. It is used when your pancreas is still able to produce a fair amount of insulin, and is able to help out at meals. This is done when your pancreas just needs a little help. It is sufficient for about half the type 2's that try it. When used as part of MDI, it is for all of your insulin needs that are not related to food intake.

Mix: if Basal only is not sufficient, mix will do more to get your glucose under control. It is simple rather than complex. It does require a schedule that is not flexible. The results are usually less than optimal, and because of the huge peak in the NPH which is part of what is used, you may experience lows at night. You have no way of adjusting how much insulin to take with meals, since you are taking rapid and long lasting insulin at the same time. What you have to do is match your carbohydrate intake to your insulin.

Multiple Daily Injections (MDI) This is the term given to the process of taking basal insulin once a day, or twice a day at about 12 hour intervals, and bolus insulin whenever you eat. To get the best results, you need to count carbohydrates and match the amount of bolus insulin to the amount of carbohydrates you are eating. It takes a while to get good at this. Once you get all the adjustments made, it is a very flexible system. You can eat meals whenever you wish, and delay or skip meals without your glucose going low. With MDI you should be trying to keep your glucose between 70 and 140 (5 and 7.8 on the measurement system used outside the United States).

Getting started on insulin

I've not spoken with anyone that likes needles. That said, they really are tiny, and the results you get, once you know what you are doing, are well worth the trouble. Diabetics should be started out with less insulin than they are expected to need, and instructed to gradually increase it (titrate the dose) until the glucose levels are brought in line. This usually takes a fair amount of time. If you get too much insulin, the effects are unpleasant at best. By going slowly, you don't overshoot. It's best to give each dose at least two days before changing it, but consult with your doctor on how often and how much to increase the dosage.

You should have your medical staff's approval beforehand for making changes.

If my insulin dosage is not right, how do I tell if it is the basal insulin or the bolus insulin that is off? This is very basic, and very important to learn. I only take bolus insulin with a meal, or to correct if I am too high. If I skip a meal or delay it long enough, then there is no bolus insulin in me. All I have left in me is basal. I test at least every half hour. If my glucose readings drift up, I am not getting enough basal insulin, if they drift down, I am getting too much. The next day, or at least the next time I am able to do basal testing, I delay or skip a different meal, and make adjustments. For many diabetics including me, the amount of basal needed during one part of the day is not the same as what is needed in another part. If you are on MDI, one thing to do that can help, is split your basal, taking half about 12 hours apart. That at least, lets you have 2 different basal rates. Not ideal, but better than just one. If description fits you, speak to your doctor about it. The best way to cover this problem of different basal needs is with an insulin pump. There you can have a change of basal rate every half hour if you need it. I'll talk about pumps in a later chapter.

Once my basal rate is set right, I can work on getting my bolus set right. I needed to work out something called insulin to carbohydrate ratio. What that term means, is how much bolus (rapid acting) insulin is needed, for a given amount of carbohydrates. Your Doctor or CDE, should give you a value to start with. If you are not insulin resistant, then one unit of insulin will likely cover at least 10 grams of carbohydrate, for some diabetics a lot more. If you have insulin resistance, it is likely that one unit will cover less than 10 grams of carbohydrate. You are usually better off getting this starting point from a CDE, or Endocrinologist, they deal with insulin on an everyday basis.

An Insulin Pen

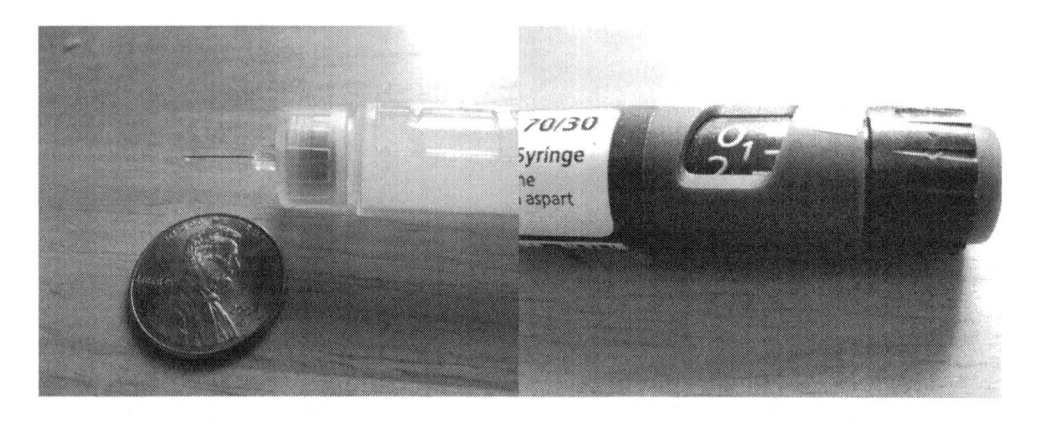

An insulin pen is a more accurate way to deliver insulin than a syringe, some pens can even deliver half units. They also tend to be more convenient to take with you when away from home.

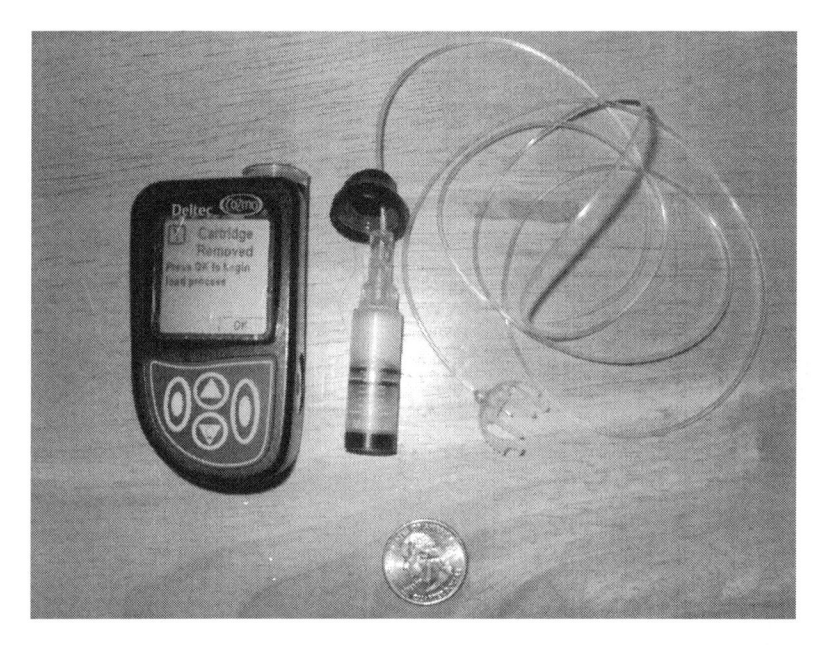

An Insulin Pump

How it works

An insulin pump delivers insulin from a cartridge mounted inside, through Teflon tubing, through a connector to a Teflon or steel cannula that extends beneath the skin. Insulin is delivered at user adjustable rates, 24 hours a day. Fast acting insulin is delivered in small amounts 24 hours a day, to mimic what would be delivered by a pancreas and as a bolus for the larger amounts needed for meals.

What does it do for you?

An insulin pump delivers insulin more accurately than a syringe or insulin pen. If you want 1.15 units of insulin, that is what you can give yourself, to the nearest twentieth of a unit or better. This is especially important for people that are very insulin sensitive and therefore take very small amounts of insulin. It can also do very small basal rates. It is also great for people who need different basal rates at different times of day, as people with Dawn Phenomenon do.

What doesn't it do?

An insulin pump does not figure out how much insulin to give you, except in the sense that it has a built in calculator and memory. Basal insulin is given at a rate you set, there can be a different rate every half hour, if that is what you need. You or your diabetes specialist, set up the schedule for how insulin is delivered. You also tell the pump how many grams of carbohydrate should receive one unit of insulin. Once you set this up, then you just tell the pump how many grams of carbohydrate you will be eating, and it calculates how much insulin to give you.

It takes quite a while to get all the settings just right, like most things with diabetes, there is plenty of trial and error. Once this is done, it is quite easy to use.

PUMPING TIPS
What this is:

This is how I do my pumping. Some things can be done successfully in more than one way, other ways are fine, as long as they work. With some things relating to pumping, there really is only one right way to do it.

Disclaimer: I make no claim that if you do things my way, you will get numbers as good as mine. I am very fortunate in that my body reacts to insulin in a very predictable way. I have been a Type 2 for 17 years, on insulin for about 5 years, and on a pump for about 4 years. I am fortunate to have the control I enjoy.

When you are just starting out:

- I suggest you buy "Pumping Insulin," by John Walsh. Just about every experienced pumper will tell you the same thing!
- Attitude is very important.
- "I'll try it" means you have a chance of succeeding.

- "I'll do whatever is needed, and learn what I have to for success" almost guarantees success.

Have reasonable expectations

- Expect that it is work getting it set up.
- Expect that it will take weeks to get numbers you are hoping for.
- Expect that things may well get worse before they get better.

There are a whole lot of things to get set right to match the insulin delivery of your pump to your body and lifestyle. That is what makes it such a powerful and flexible tool. With every change you make, you need to go look at the results, and decide if that is an improvement or not, and if you have reached your goal for that particular limit. I have 15 basal rates, due to Dawn Phenomenon, it took 6 weeks to tweak the settings on my pump to the point where I was happy with the results.

It is well worth, the time and effort!

Infusion sets

I highly recommend getting free samples, so you can try different types out to see what works for you. When you buy infusion sets, you are usually buying 10 of them, so if you don't like them you will be stuck with them for a month. A few phone calls and e-mails got me a months worth of samples of various kinds.

Good carbohydrate counting skill is a necessity!

Lowering your carbohydrate intake will improve your control, because your errors in carbohydrate estimation will be smaller.

An example to illustrate:

An omelet for breakfast, 4 grams of carbohydrate. A 25% error in carbohydrate estimation would mean an error of 1 gram of carbohydrate.

An omelet, toast, juice, and a huge plate of hash browns, 100 grams of carbs. A 25% error in carbohydrate estimation would be 25 grams of carbohydrate.

Your test 2 hrs after eating the second breakfast could be 25 times as far from your target number as it would be from eating the first one.

Some pumping rules I live by:

1. Indicate to the pump when you disconnect, that way it will remind you if you forget to reconnect!

2. When changing pump settings, make small changes.

3. When changing pump settings, change one thing at time!

4. Verify that the changes are what you intended! You could hurt yourself with a mistake. Verify that the changes you made are working! What if you screwed up, and moved a value in the wrong direction, or too far?

5. Double check for user error BEFORE replacing a set.

Forgetting to bolus, or not giving the bolus for the whole meal, or if you take pills, forgetting your pills happens much more often than a problem with the pump or infusion set. Check the log on the pump, it will tell you what the pump was told to do.

6. If you have a problem with glucose that is too high, bad insulin is one of the first things you may think of, but it is the least likely thing to be the problem. Unless you freeze the insulin, or cook it by forgetting it in the car in hot weather, your insulin will most likely be fine.

7. I do not change infusion sets right before bed. If something goes wrong, either I will not know about it, or I will be up half the night worrying about it if I do notice there is a problem.

8. Keep a spare battery for the pump with you or in your vehicle.

9. Use insulin that is at room temperature. This prevents air bubbles from forming, moreover cold insulin could be painful.

10. I take the time to get all the bubbles out, when changing insulin.

11. I have my pump set to remind me to test 2 hours after a bolus, including correction boluses.

12. I don't try to keep the changing of infusion sets and insulin cartridges synchronized. If you keep them synchronized, you are likely tossing out perfectly good insulin.

13. It is a good idea if you add up all the basal insulin that will be delivered while you are sleeping. That way you know what minimum amount has to be left in the pump before you go to sleep. Add that amount to what the minimum is for the "low insulin" alarm. Who wants to be awakened at 3:00 AM for pump messages about being low on insulin?

14. A trick that will significantly lower your average glucose. Lets say, for example, you have a target of 90 (this works, whatever target you set). I test, and my glucose meter says 99. Not bad, but you I make it better by doing a correction. Many pumps will figure this out, but if not you can still get very close if you know your correction factor. That is how many points will you drop for each unit of insulin you take. I know I drop 11 points if I take 1 unit, so if I wanted to drop from 99 to 90, 1 unit would get me to 88. If I was doing it in my head, that is close enough. Even to the nearest quarter unit, is an improvement, but if I let the pump do the calculation, I will end up right on target.

15. I rotate placement of your infusion sites, so they have plenty of time to heal before they get used again.

Shortcuts that work, to save money. Tubing can be reused at least twice times. I do that at least enough to have spare tubing at hand, in case I catch my tubing on a doorknob and damage it.

16. Insulin will last longer than the 48 hours in a pump that the spec sheets say. I always do at least 3 days, this saves on cartridges. I have never had any problem with the insulin.

17. There is a potential problem in leaving sets in place longer than 3 days. Some people have problems with scar tissue forming, so they have areas that can no longer used for infusion sets. I just can't see taking that risk. After about 3 days, your body starts to react to the infusion site, time to remove the cannula. I want to be able to pump for the rest of my life, until something better comes along, or there is a cure, without having to put the set in a less desirable place than I now use.

How often should you change your infusion set? I asked this question on an online forum.

This is a summary of the responses in an online poll I took:

3 days 10 responses

3-4 days 4 responses

Here is what people experienced if they left the site in longer:
- Redness
- Infections
- Absorption Issues
- Scar Tissue

Pay attention to cold weather, you will burn carbohydrates at a much more rapid rate. Temporary basal is appropriate if you are going to be outdoors in the winter for extended periods.

Pump Batteries

I tested a number of batteries in my cozmo pump for real life usage duration. My pump uses 1 AAA battery.

I am a very heavy battery user, I am a type 2 so I pump large amounts of insulin, I use alarms, and I use back lighting. The only battery intensive feature I don't use is vibrate. So, consider this a worst case, you will likely get longer.

EverReady Lithium....................13 days

EverReady Titanium...................6 days

Duracell..5 days

EverReady Energizer..................5 days

Rayovac..5 days

"Our family" house brand............5 days

The thing about lithium batteries is they maintain full voltage until almost the end of their life, so your battery meter in the pump won't give you a true indication of their life remaining. From the first indication that it is not "full," to the alarm that it is almost dead, is about 3 or 4 hours. So, if you are Type1 and a heavy sleeper, this might not be for you. As a T2 and a lite sleeper, I don't worry about it.

INFUSION SETS

An infusion set is what connects an insulin pump, to you. It consists of a small Teflon tube or a needle that is mated to a connector that you stick to your skin, and Teflon tubing that goes from the connector to an insulin pump. Connector type MM is Medtronic Minimed and Luer is for non-medronic pumps.

Use of the Thinset Reservoir allows Luer lock sets to be used with minimed pumps.

- Set name **Cleo**
- Insertion Angle 90
- Cannula Type Teflon
- Cannula lengths 6, 9 mm
- Tube Lengths 24, 31 inches
- Insertion Method Automatic
- Connector Type Luer
- Disconnect Yes
- Strongest Features: 360 rotation
- Some people won't want to use this because: automatic insertion only
- Sold by: Animas
- Sold by: Smiths Medical

- Set Name **Contact Detach**
- Insertion Angle 90
- Cannula Type Needle
- Cannula lengths 6, 8 mm
- Tube Lengths 24, 31 inches
- Insertion Method Manual
- Connector Type Luer
- Disconnect Yes
- Strongest Features One hand insertion
- Some people won't want to use this because: Needle remains in you until you remove the set.
- Sold by:Animas
- Made By: Unimedical
- Note: The Contact Detach, Rapid D, and Sure-T are all the same set, just different connectors

- Set name **Contact**
- Insertion Angle 90
- Cannula Type Needle
- Cannula lengths 6, 8, 10 mm
- Tube Lengths 23, 31, 43 inches
- Insertion Method Manual
- Connector Type Luer Disconnect No
- Strongest Features One hand insertion

- Some people won't want to use this because: Needle remains in you until you remove the set
- Sold by:Animas
- Made By: Unimedical

- Set name **Comfort Short**
- Insertion Angle 10-45
- Cannula Type Teflon
- Cannula lengths 13 mm
- Tube Lengths 23, 43 inches
- Insertion Method Manual
- Connector Type Luer
- Disconnect Yes
- Strongest Features: Large adhesive area
- Some people won't want to use this because: Manual insertion only
- Sold by: Animas
- Sold by: Smiths Medical
- Made By: Unimedical

- Set name **Comfort**
- Insertion Angle 10-45
- Cannula Type Teflon
- Cannula lengths 17 mm
- Tube Lengths 23, 31, 43 inches

- Insertion Method Manual
- Connector Type Luer
- Disconnect Yes
- Strongest Features: Large adhesive area
- Some people won't want to use this because: Manual insertion only
- Sold by: Animas
- Sold by: Smiths Medical
- Made By: Unimedical
- Note: The Silhouette, Tender, and Comfort are all the same sets, just different connectors

Set name **Inset**

- Insertion Angle 90
- Cannula Type Teflon
- Cannula lengths 6, 9 mm
- Tube Lengths 23, 43 inches
- Insertion Method Automatic
- Connector Type Luer
- Disconnect Yes
- Strongest Features One Hand Insertion
- Sold by: Animas
- Made by: Unimedical

- Set name **Orbit 90**
- Insertion Angle 90
- Cannula Type Teflon
- Cannula 6, 9 mm
- Tube Lengths 24, 31, 42 inches
- Insertion Method Manual
- Connector Disconnect Yes
- Strongest Features 360 degree rotation, one hand insertion
- Some people won't want to use this because: Manual insertion
- Made By: ICU Medical

- Set name **Polyfin**
- Insertion Angle 30
- Cannula Type Bent Needle
- Cannula lengths 15 mm
- Tube Lengths 24 inches
- Insertion Method Manual
- Connector Type Luer
- Disconnect Yes
- Some people won't want to use this because: Needle remains in you until you remove the set
- Sold by: Animas
- Sold by: Medtronic

- Set name **Quickset**
- Insertion Angle 90
- Cannula Type Teflon
- Cannula lengths 6, 9 mm
- Tube Lengths 23 43 inches
- Insertion Method Manual, OR Automatic
- Connector Type MM
- Disconnect Yes
- Strongest Features Simple and easy to use
- Sold by:Animas
- Sold by: Medtronic
- Made By: Unimedical

- Set name **Rapid D**
- Insertion Angle 90
- Cannula Type Needle
- Cannula lengths 6, 8 mm
- Tube Lengths 24, 43 inches
- Insertion Method Manual
- Connector Type Luer
- Disconnect Yes
- Strongest Features one hand insertion
- Sold by: Animas

- Made By: Unimedical
- Note: The Contact Detach, Rapid D, and Sure-T are all the same set, just different connectors

- Set name **Silhouette**
- Insertion Angle 10-45
- Cannula Type Teflon
- Cannula lengths 13, 17 mm
- Tube Lengths 23, 43 inches
- Insertion Method Manual or Automatic
- Connector Type, MM
- Disconnect Yes
- Strongest Features Good for lean children or kids
- Some people won't want to use this because: long needle looks scary, Silserter is "pure torture" and guarantees a kink, says one user
- Sold by:Animas
- Sold by: Medtronic
- Note: The Silhouette, Tender, and Comfort are all the same sets

- Set name **SimpleChoice Eas**y
- Insertion Angle 30
- Cannula Type Teflon
- Cannula lengths 12, 17 mm
- Tube Lengths 23, 43 inches
- Insertion Method Manual or Automatic
- Connector Type Luer Disconnect Yes
- Strongest Features Very large adhesive area
- Sold by:Animas

- Set name **SimpleChoice Easy Pro**
- Insertion Angle 30
- Cannula Type Teflon
- Cannula lengths 12, 17 mm
- Tube Lengths 23, 43 inches
- Insertion Method Manual or Automatic
- Connector Type, MM
- Disconnect Yes
- Strongest Features Very large adhesive area

- Set name **Simplechoice Twist**
- Insertion Angle 90
- Cannula Type Teflon
- Cannula lengths 5, 9 mm
- Tube Lengths 23. 43 inches
- Insertion Method Manual
- Connector Type Luer
- Disconnect Yes
- Strongest Features 360 degree rotation at site
- Some people won't want to use this because: Manual insertion only

- Set name **Simplechoice Twist Pro**
- Insertion Angle 90
- Cannula Type Teflon
- Cannula lengths 5, 9 mm
- Tube Lengths 23, 43 inches
- Insertion Method Manual
- Connector Type, MM
- Disconnect Yes
- Strongest Features 360 degree rotation at site
- Some people won't want to use this because: Manual insertion only

- Set name **Sof-set Micro**
- Insertion Angle 90
- Cannula Type Teflon
- Cannula lengths 6 mm
- Tube Lengths 24, 42 inches
- Insertion Method Manual Or Automatic
- Connector Type, MM
- Disconnect Yes
- Some people won't want to use this because: Requires extra tape
- Sold by: Animas

- Set name **Sof-set Ultimate**
- Insertion Angle 90
- Cannula Type Teflon
- Cannula lengths 9 mm
- Tube Lengths 42 inches
- Insertion Method Manual, or Automatic
- Connector Type, MM
- Disconnect Yes
- Some people won't want to use this because: Requires extra tape

- Set name **Sure-T**
- Insertion Angle 90
- Cannula Type Needle
- Cannula lengths 6
- Tube Lengths 23
- Connector Type, MM
- Disconnect Yes
- Strongest Features No cannula means no kinks
- Some people won't want to use this because: only come with 23" tubing, but silhouette tubing works okay
- Sold by: Medtronic
- Note: The Contact Detach, Rapid D, and Sure-T are all the same set, just different connectors

- Set name **Tender Mini**
- Insertion Angle 10-45
- Cannula Type Teflon
- Cannula lengths 13 17
- Tube Lengths 24, 31, 43 inches
- Insertion Method Manual
- Connector Type Luer
- Disconnect Yes
- Sold by: Animas

- Set name **Tender**
- Insertion Angle 30-45
- Cannula Type Teflon
- Cannula lengths 17 mm
- Tube Lengths 24, 31, 43 inches
- Insertion Method Manual
- Connector Type Luer
- Disconnect Yes
- Sold by: Animas

MAKING PUMP ADJUSTMENTS

Lets say you have just started pumping, but your glucose numbers vary all over the place. How do you straighten things out? Here is how I do it.

Step one is get the basal rate set right. The thing to remember is you have one way to separate problems with basal, from problems with bolus. That is, during a specific time, don't eat, and don't bolus. What is left is your basal insulin.

Morning is the place I start, because I have already fasted. I skip breakfast, and if I need to, I can move lunch up, say to 11:00 AM.

There is an alternative, I like bacon and eggs, it is a great alternative to skipping a meal. It takes 5 eggs to equal 1 gram of carbohydrate, and none at all in bacon. So, as long as I don't eat anything else that has carbohydrate (including drink), I am fine. Coffee can affect your glucose. Here is how I adjust my basal rates.

I test every half hour, from 6:00 AM to 11:00 AM. I look for a pattern. If my glucose is drifting up, then I am going to need a little more insulin. If I am drifting down, I need a little less. The trick here is, I need to schedule the change in basal for about an hour before I want it to be in place. For example: if I have steady glucose until 9 am, then it starts to rise, that means I need to increase my basal rate at about 8 am. Not a lot, a little at a time.

The next day (or next time I do adjustments), I eat an early breakfast, say 6 or 7 am and bolus for it. By 11:00 AM, the food and the bolus insulin should be out of my system. I delay lunch until 2:00 PM. Now I can check to see how my basal is doing between 11 am and 2:00 PM, and make adjustments as needed. The next time, I could have a late breakfast at 10 am or an early lunch at 10 am, and by 2:00 PM the food and bolus would be out of my system, so I can check the 2:00 PM to 6:00 PM period. In this way, I can work my way through the day, a little bit at a time until I get the right basal rates set.

Once my basal is set right, I need to work on my carbohydrate-to-insulin ratio. I need to know how many grams of carbohydrate need one gram of insulin.

There are several ways to this, they all require trial and error. A starting point comes from your pump trainer. What I do is start with less insulin than I expect to need. Too little insulin is not hard to correct. Too much insulin is usually unpleasant.

Another number that has to be entered in the pump is your correction factor. That is how many points will one unit drop your glucose. I test at different times of the day, by giving myself one unit of insulin at a time when my glucose is stable. I note how far my glucose drops by testing every half hour starting at 60 minutes until it is stable. Once I know that 1 unit drops me 11 points, then my pump can do the calculations for a correction by dividing how high my glucose is above my stated goal, by 11, to get the answer in units to be given. Some pumps will even help you when you are low, telling you how many grams of carbohydrate you need to eat.

To keep tight control, I readjust these numbers when I notice that after a meal I am ending up consistently higher or lower than before a meal. If I am ending up lower than before the meal, I am getting too much insulin, and I need to have one unit cover more carbohydrates. If you download your numbers from your pump or glucose meter to a computer, it can be quite revealing when your settings are off, just from the averages. I make small changes, and look at my results.

This is part science, part art, and part experience. Write things down! It takes accurate pump settings, and accurate carbohydrate counting to get things working smoothly.

Most pumps have reminders you can set, to change your insulin set, to test 2 hours after a bolus, and reminders you can set if you take pills. This last one can be really important to Type 2's, we often have many pills to take.

Standard Deviation

Less deviation is better

Standard Deviation, often abbreviated SD, is a measure of glucose variability, and is usually obtained from insulin pumps, and from some glucose meters (including cgms). It can also come from the programs that the meters and pumps upload their data to. What are we measuring here? We are measuring how tightly packed your readings are around your average, or to state the opposite, how widely scattered they are.

If you bounce all day from high to low and back, that will show up as a high standard deviation. If you are very stable, without many highs or lows, that will show up as a very low SD.

The lower the number the better.

What is a good number? Under half your average glucose for a type 1.

As a type 2, I have found that I am able to do much better than that. I started pumping at an SD of about 25 mg/dl (1.4 mmol). Now my SD is 14 mg/dl (.83 mmol).

If your average is made up from a 250 (13.9) and a 50 (2.8) it averages 150 (8.3). The 150 (8.3) average is not bad, but the 50 (2.8) is too low and the 250 (13.9) is too high. If you only look at the average, you might think you are doing well, when you are not doing so well.

Looking at a standard deviation will tell you if your average is made up of good numbers(great), or high numbers and low numbers averaging themselves out (not good).

Blood Tests

What is an A1c?

An A1c test is a weighted average, which represents what your glucose has been for the past 3 months. How do you take a test that tells you the past, rather than the present? It is a very clever test. The full name is hemoglobin A1c.

Some of your red blood cells have glucose attached to them. The more glucose in your blood, the more red blood cells get glucose attached. Once a glucose attaches, it stays attached. So why 3 months? Because that is how long red blood cells last, before your body replaces them. They are not replaced evenly over the 3 months though, about half are replaced in the most recent month. That is why the test is a weighted average.

What is a good number?

So, what are good results and what are bad results for an A1c test? It is generally considered that if your results are 8% or greater, your diabetes is out of control. 7% to 8% is mediocre. The ADA has set a goal of less than 7%.

Also, they consider 5.7 to 6.4% to indicate levels in the pre-diabetic range.

Normal for a non-diabetic varies from lab to lab, mine considers normal to be 4.7 to 5.8. I am very happy with my current A1c of 5.0, and the fact that my last 16 A1c tests have been at 5.4 % or lower.

Why does it matter?

The Diabetes control and complications trial (DCCT)

Conducted from 1983 to 1993 by the National Institute of Diabetes and Digestive and Kidney Diseases, this study showed that keeping your glucose close to normal slowed the progression of microvascular complications (eye, kidney and nerve damage). The study was done on 1441 Type 1 volunteers, in the United States and Canada, ages 13 to 39. The volunteers had Type 1 for one to 15 years.

Here are the results of the study, in brief:

- Intensive blood glucose control reduces the risk of eye disease by 76%
- Kidney Disease 50%
- Nerve disease 60%.
- Any cardiovascular disease event 42%
- Nonfatal heart attack, stroke, or death from cardiovascular causes 57%

UK Prospective Diabetes Study (UKPDS)

This was a 20 year study of more than 5,000 type 2 diabetics. The findings in brief: intensive control reduces:

- Major eye disease by a quarter
- Early Kidney damage by a third
- Strokes by more than a third
- Serious deterioration of vision by more than a third

Here is my evaluation:

These studies compared A1c's in the 7's with 8's, 9's, and 10's. In the 7's was considered good control.

I don't consider 7 to 8% to be very good control (more like mediocre). There really is no data on people who keep their A1c's in the 5's.

I figure, 5% is about the glucose a non-diabetic has. If I can keep mine in the same range, that is the best chance I have for avoiding complications. I have no complications so far, after 17 years of diabetes.

What I find most convincing about these 2 studies, is the fact that you get almost the same results from looking at Type 1 and Type 2 diabetics. Different causes for different types of diabetes, but the number of complications is dependent on how high your glucose is for both types.

Other test results matter too, but A1c is at the top of my list. Values given are for the USA:

Vitamin D

Type 2's often have a problem with often being low on vitamin D. More is better, but only up to a point

- Normal 30-100 ng/mL
- Deficiency less than 10 ng/mL
- Insufficiency 10-30 ng/mL
- Sufficiency 30 - 100 ng/mL
- Toxicity greater than 100 ng/mL

Fasting Glucose

This is a chance for you to check on the accuracy of your meter. If you test with your meter shortly before or after your blood draw, and write down the result, you can compare with the lab results.

Thyroid

A TSH value 0.34 to 4.82 is normal at my lab

Cholesterol

- Total 0 - 200 Normal at my lab
- LDL 0 - 135 Normal at my lab
- HDL 40 - 60 Normal at my lab (for males)
-

Triglycerides

Normal is 30 - 150 mg/dl

In a type 2, excess glucose is turned in to Triglycerides. If you get your glucose under control, Triglycerides will usually also be in control.

Gad 65 antibodies

Normal is less than 5.0

This is a test for signs that your pancreas has been attacked by your autoimmune system. High numbers indicate type 1 diabetes.

C-peptide

What is c-peptide

C-Peptide is a leftover, from when insulin is made in your pancreas. For each insulin molecule made, there is one c-peptide made. Since modern injected insulin does not have c-peptide, a measurement of c-peptide will give a measurement of how much insulin your pancreas is making, even if you are injecting or infusing insulin. C-Peptide does not last as long as insulin in your blood, so they have to take that into account. This is one of the tests used to distinguish Type 1 from Type 2. Producing more than the normal amount of insulin is a type 2 characteristic. Producing very little insulin is a type 1 characteristic, but also happens to a type 2 who is injecting or infusing insulin.

MY WELL RESTED PANCREAS

I am 60, a Type 2 for 17 years, on a pump for 4 years. I recently learned that one of the requirements for having an insulin pump and supplies paid for by medicare at age 65, is that your c-peptide must be no higher than 110% of the minimum at your lab, and this test must be done while your glucose is 225 or higher. At my lab the minimum is 0.8. Type 1's do not have this requirement. You have to have the tests done at a hospital, and you have to meet these conditions only once and have the results on file.

I had a c-peptide test done a year ago, my c-peptide was 0.2 while my glucose was about 80. C-peptide done that way shows my pancreas is producing very little insulin (I have had Type 1 friends say they were 0.2 when diagnosed).

The following test shows how much my pancreas can produce rather than what it normally produces, by insuring my pancreas is getting the signal to produce all it can. This is done by removing external sources of insulin, at a time when you have high glucose.

Rather than worry about it for 5 years, I decided to have the test done early.

5 years ago:

My A1c went from 7.1 to 8.7 in 3 months, after 12 years of oral medications. It was clear they would no longer suffice. I started injections, but still had fasting glucose of 200 to 250, with occasional numbers as high as 350 due to Dawn Phenomenon.

Present day:

I eat 80 grams of carbohydrate a day, and my glucose seldom goes over 140 for meal peaks.

The night before the test I consumed large amounts of carbohydrates, to the tune of 350 to 400 grams. I was hoping to get my glucose high enough that my dawn phenomenon would insure that I was still over 225 by 8:00 AM test time (it is a fasting test).I went in to my doctors office for the c-peptide and fasting glucose tests that morning.

I did not bolus for lunch the previous day, and removed the pump at 2:00 PM.

CLEARLY, the 3 years rest my pancreas had while the pump did all the work, has done my pancreas good.

My fasting glucose was **204**, and the c-peptide was **5.9**.

My fasting readings before I went on insulin (5 years ago) were usually **200-250**, with readings as high as **350**.

I conclude that my pancreas is more capable than it was 5 years ago. Without having Actos now, which I was taking back then, when I try to raise my glucose to 250 I cannot. There is no way of knowing how long my pancreas could keep up this pace. I have reason to believe that if I stopped infusing insulin, in a matter of months I would be back where I was 5 years ago, with high fasting readings. It is interesting to speculate what might have happened if I had gone on insulin 12 years earlier. Interesting to think about, but the fact is I was not ready for insulin and would have resisted if it were offered.

I'll leave it to the reader to draw their own conclusions about their own condition.

Here is the log, you can see how hard I tried to raise my glucose, and if you look at my numbers you can see how valiantly my pancreas fought to bring the glucose under control. This is totally different from when I am using the pump, in that case the pump does all the work. My glucose never gets high enough for my pancreas to be triggered to make insulin.

12:00 Lunch, 25 grams of carbohydrate, potatoes, chicken, salad NO Bolus

1:00 PM 113

1:52 PM 128

2:00 PM removed pump

3:08 PM 141

4:15 PM 108

5:58 PM 104

6:00 PM Spaghetti dinner 114 grams of carbohydrate

6:30 PM 55 grams of carbohydrate, ice cream

6:36 PM 125

6:55 PM 132

7:17 PM 132

7:30 PM 18 grams of carbohydrate mini tacos

7:36 PM 137

7:45 PM 137

8:00 PM to 8:15PM 6 cups popcorn

8:18 PM 157

8:29 PM 152

8:44PM 162

9:02 PM 161

9:04 PM 8 grams of carbohydrate (glucose tabs)

9:16 PM 162

9:30PM 16 grams of carbohydrate (taco shells)

9:36 PM 205

9:47 PM 182

9:58 PM 16 grams of carbohydrate taco shells

10:00 PM 182

10:07 PM 16 grams of carbohydrate, taco shells

10:15 PM 175

10:38 PM 152

10:45 PM 10 grams of carbohydrate, apple juice + 3 teaspoon sugar

11:10 PM 177

11:23 PM 16 grams of carbohydrate (glucose tabs)

11:37 PM 199

12:20 AM 219

Medical Exams

Eye, Foot, and Dental Exams

Why are they so critical?

Diabetics often have problems with their immune system, this can lead to problems in fighting infections. They also can have nerve damage, and they do not always feel pain, especially in their feet. These two things combine to lead to infected sores that they don't even know are there.

Calluses can turn into ulcers. Care must be taken, though tight glucose control lessens the risks.

Diabetes is the leading cause of blindness in adults 20 to 74. Your eyes are one of the first things to be affected and need to be checked at least once a year.

Diabetics have a larger incidence of tooth decay, periodontal disease, salivary gland disfunction, and fungal infection than non diabetics. Keeping your glucose close to what a non-diabetic would have helps reduce the likelihood of these problems occurring.

Will my Diabetes get Worse?

That is one of the more common questions I get asked. The answer depends on two things, what you mean by worse, and what you plan to do to prevent it.

Type one diabetics sometimes have some insulin production still happening at the time they are diagnosed. They are in what is called a "honeymoon phase," or they have a "sputtering pancreas," (it works some of the time). Before long, this insulin production is diminished or stopped altogether. This is called progression, and it happens in a few days to a few years.

For type 2 diabetics, progression usually takes longer, a few years to decades. Sometimes at the start, reducing the amount of carbohydrates you eat and adding exercise is enough to bring your glucose down to acceptable levels. In time, your pancreas produces less insulin and quite often insulin resistance gets worse. Additional oral medications are needed, and usually insulin will be needed at some point. The thing to remember is that the outcome of avoiding microvascular complications (damage to your eyes, nerves, and kidneys) is what we strive for. Diabetes does not cause these complications directly. Diabetes raises glucose, and high glucose causes the complications. Why is this an important distinction? If you take steps to get your glucose in line, chances of having complications fall to about the same rate as non-diabetics have. If you don't keep your glucose levels low, then the likelihood of complications will greatly increase. Complications take a while to happen, depending on how high your glucose is. Once they start to develop, there is not much you can do about them except keep things from getting worse. The damage has already started, and much of that damage is not reversible. There seems to be a window of opportunity to get help correcting nerve damage, up to the point where the nerve dies.

In my case, I went from pills to more pills to insulin, but I also went from A1c's in the 7's to A1c's in the 5's with insulin. Did my diabetes get worse? Well, it certainly progressed, my pancreas is capable of producing less insulin than 17 years ago, but a bit more insulin than it could 5 years ago, as shown by my c-peptide test. It recovered some due to the rest it is getting, since my pump is doing almost all the work. My control now is great, and my chances of having complications has gone to almost nil. I don't consider my diabetes to have become worse, I think it is in better shape than it was. The effort needed to achieve this is greater, and the level of knowledge needed is greater.

After 4 years on an insulin pump, my pancreas has recovered some of it's ability to produce insulin. Not enough to do without the pump though. I did not start on insulin until I had been on oral medications for 12 years. I think Type 2's are better off starting on insulin sooner rather than later. The recovery might be enough to be able go get by with a minimum of insulin help or in some cases metformin only, after help from insulin has rested your pancreas for a while.

If you mean will you need to take more in the future, than you do now? That can be, if you get more insulin resistance, of if you gain weight so you have more blood, or if some areas that you use to inject or infuse insulin develop scar tissue.

Travel

The container for this kit cost about $9.00 at Walmart, it is handy for traveling.

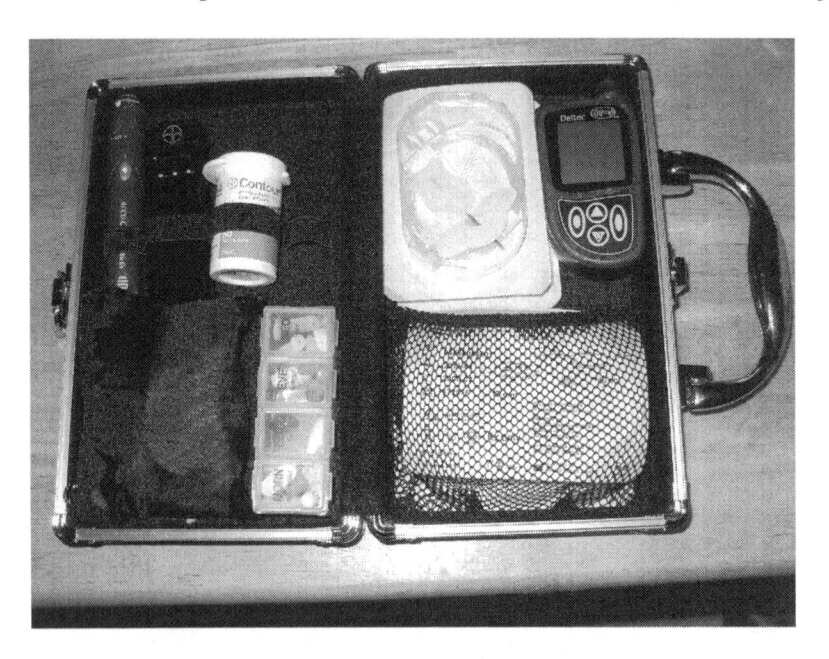

I strongly suggest you make a list of what diabetes gear you plan to take with you on a trip. If you have enough spares, packing at your own pace ahead of time instead of the last minute reduces the amount of forgotten items.

Cooling insulin while traveling

There are really 2 levels of cooling to think about. Insulin can go bad at temperatures warmer than 86 degrees Fahrenheit. You need to keep your opened insulin cooled to at least this level. For travel or camping there are coolers such as the Frio, which work by evaporation. This keeps the insulin cool, but not cold. They are ideal for this use. Insulin that is opened, or cooled this way, can only be counted on to be good for about a month.

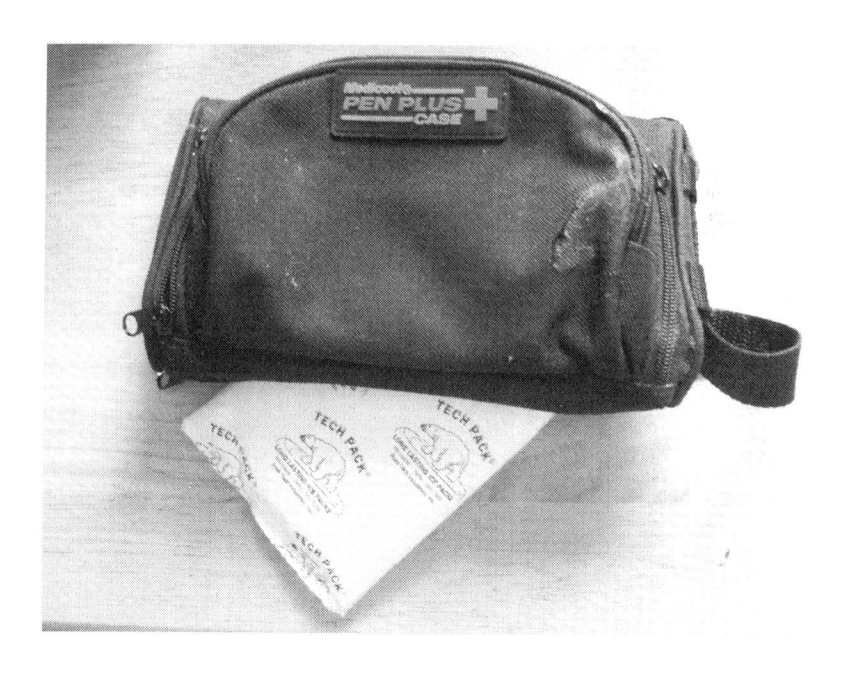

Insulin saved for future use, needs to be refrigerated. At refrigerator temperatures, insulin will keep for more than a year. For this use, they make insulin Wallets that have a section with a jell pack that you freeze. This will keep the insulin cold.

Insulin can be kept in a cooler with ice, but you need to make sure the insulin is in a container so that it will not freeze, because that would destroy the insulin. The insulin must not touch the ice. You could also use plastic "blue ice" in a cooler. I have often used a cooler that plugs into a car cigarette lighter. It will cool both drinks and insulin.

Future Technologies

Noninvasive glucose monitoring

Possible methods under development
- Contact lenses that change color with your glucose
- Infra red light on your arm
- Electromagnetic sensor
- Scanning your eye

Don't hold your breath, but many possible methods are under development.

Artificial Pancreas

What is it? The most common approach is a combination of a continuous glucose monitor and an insulin pump, with an algorithm (software) to control the two. Often a glucagon pump is used in combination with an insulin pump. The goal is a pump that adjusts itself to your life. It will be available eventually, but likely a little at a time. Slowly and carefully pumps will get smarter.

Low Carbohydrate Treats

Sugar Free Peanut Butter Cookies

- 1 cup peanut butter (crunchy seems to work best)
- 1 egg (or one-fourth cup eggbeater)
- 1 teaspoon vanilla
- 1 cup splenda
- One-fourth cup almond flour (makes the cookies less fragile)

Mix together well and roll into balls as you would regular peanut butter cookies. Press with a fork dipped into water then splenda, making a cross pattern on top of each cookie. Bake at 350 degrees for 10 to 18 minutes until browned.

Low carbohydrate pancakes

- 2 large eggs
- One-fourth cup splenda
- 1 tablespoon vanilla extract
- 1 one-fourth cup water
- 1 and one-half cups almond flour
- One-half teaspoon sea salt
- One-half teaspoon baking soda
- 2 tbsp grape seed oil

In a blender, combine the eggs, splenda, vanilla extract, and water; mix on high for about 1 minute, until smooth. Add the almond flour, salt, baking soda, and blend until thoroughly combined.

Heat the grape seed oil in a large skillet over medium-low heat. Ladle 1 heaping tablespoon of the batter onto the skillet for each pancake. Cook until small bubbles form on the top of each pancake; when the bubbles begin to open, flip each pancake. When fully cooked, transfer the pancakes to a plate.

Repeat the process with the remaining batter, then serve.

One-fourth cup of almond flour has 4 grams of carbohydrate, one-fourth cup of all purpose white flour has about 23 grams

Frequently Asked Questions

Q. Is there a way to avoid eating too many of your favorite berries?

A Eat them frozen, that is self limiting.

Q Should I avoid high carbohydrate foods, or high sugar foods?

A Both. Sugar is a form of carbohydrate.

Q I like to drink beer. Do I need to stop, now that I am a type 2?

A Be aware of the carbohydrates, about 3 for a lite beer, and about 12 for a regular.

Q When I inject Lantus, I feel a burning sensation. Is that normal?

A Lantus is more acetic than your skin. Larger doses burn more. Splitting the dosage helps, injecting slowly can also help.

Q I just started on insulin, should I quit my Glyburide and Metformin?

A You will need to speak with your doctor. Metformin will reduce the amount of insulin you need.

Q I have heard that testing on your finger is more accurate than testing on your arm. Is that true?

A Yes and No. Blood circulates more rapidly to your fingers, so glucose measured from your fingers will show changes more rapidly than blood from your arm. This means at times when your glucose is changing rapidly, like after a meal or during exercise, your fingers might be a better choice. At times when your glucose is stable, testing on your arm might be a good choice, because there are fewer nerve endings on your arm so you are less likely to hit a nerve and have it be painful.

Q I forgot my Metformin at home, and am at work and about to eat lunch, what should I do?

A If you realize you forgot to bring metformin to work, and lunch is not yet planned, you could go easy on the carbohydrates, and get a salad. Metformin helps with carbohydrates, so don't eat as many.

A good idea for the future, is to keep some metformin in your car, coat, jacket, purse, desk, or locker as spare. I take the maximum dosage, and I find that if I miss it at lunch I am about 30 points higher 2 hours later than if I took it. It's one of those things where an exception is not going to mess you up, but you need to be in the habit of taking it. Just a reminder, I am on insulin, likely metformin matters a bit less for those who do not use insulin.

Q People sometimes find that splitting their Lantus dose in two parts, 12 hours apart, helps. Why?

A You can split the dose unevenly if you need to, also you have less trouble if lantus runs out in less than 24 hours. Also higher doses of lantus sting, since the acidity is different from your skin. Splitting it into 2 doses makes it burn less.

Q Which is better for a diabetic, counting calories or counting carbohydrates?

A If your goal is to lose weight, counting calories is likely to work a little better. Counting carbohydrates is more likely to offer help in controlling your glucose, and thus your diabetes complications. Counting carbohydrates also provides some weight loss, because carbohydrates have a large amount of calories, so reducing them is likely to also reduce your calories.

Q Should I test my glucose after one or two hours after eating?

A Testing two hours after eating is done because that is about the amount of time usually needed for a type 2 to return to the glucose level you had before eating. Testing at 1 hour also has it's uses, that is usually about the time you reach your peak glucose from eating. Testing then will let you see how much various foods raise your glucose.

Q Will I be able to stop taking my medicines if I lose weight?

A That sometimes happens, and it sometimes happens you don't need as many of them or that smaller doses are enough. How much weight you loose, how much exercise you do, and how long you have had diabetes all factor into it. The less time since diagnosis, the more likely you would be to be able to get by without oral medicines.

Q How accurate are glucose meters?

A They are built to be plus or minus 20% but are usually within 5% or 10% of a true reading.

Q What can I use as justifications for an insulin pump, when discussing with it my insurance company?

A The need to take very small amounts of insulin, being hypoglycemic unaware, and the presence of Dawn Phenomenon are 3 good justifications.

Q Which diet works better for a diabetic, low carbohydrate or low fat diet?

A If you don't have insulin resistance, they both work, with low carbohydrate usually working a little better. Low carbohydrate is easier on your heart. The more insulin resistance you have, the better the low carb choice is.

Q Is type 2 Diabetes always progressive?

A If it is caught in its early stages (pre-diabetic), then exercise and a reduction in carbohydrates can sometimes lead to remission. That is, being able to get by without medication. That is not a cure, because returning to your former lifestyle would lead to high glucose again. The normal thing for type two, is for your pancreas to lose working beta cells as time goes on. This does not necessarily mean you will have complications, but you will need to change the ways you manage your diabetes.

Q Are artificial sweeteners safe?

A Yes. Do they contain carbohydrates? Usually only one per serving.

Q Can insulin lose its effectiveness?

A That is a tricky multipart question, though it does not look like it. Insulin can lose it's effectiveness if it gets too warm, or if it is stored for more than 28 days after being opened. It is ruined completely if frozen.

If you mean, will there come a time that insulin will no longer work for you? The best answer I can give is my friend Richard has been taking it for 65 years!

Q What should your fasting numbers be?

A I am on insulin, and aim for 90 to 105. On pills, there is less you can do about your fasting numbers. A Type 1 would likely not try to keep fasting as low as I do, because their glucose is more volatile.

Q I started on insulin a week ago, but my numbers are not going down. Why?

A When you start on insulin, your health care provider has you start with less insulin than you are expected to need, then gradually increase the dosage (titrate) until the right dosage is found. You most likely won't see much change until a few days before the right dosage. If you need 20 units, the results from taking 15 units won't look much different from the results from taking 13 units.

Q Can beta cells regenerate?

A For a diabetic, to a very limited extent.

Before going on insulin, my fasting glucose would be 200 to 250 every morning. Now, I disconnected my pump for 20 hours, and tried to get my glucose maximized for a test, and 219 was the highest I could get it. That is after 1 year of injections, and 4 of pumping. Was that regeneration, or just better functioning of what I have? I'm not sure, but my pancreas is doing a better job for sure. Not good enough to do without insulin, however.

Q I am on the highway, and I don't have time for anything but a quick grab and go at fast food somewhere. Can you suggest something that would at least be better than a burger?

A Chicken Nuggets It is the hamburger bun that causes the big rise in glucose, the rise from nuggets is not that much. If you are not doing the driving, a salad to go would be a good thing.

Q I am uninsured, where can I go to get relatively cheap diabetes supplies?

A Walmart. Their Relion brand of meters and strips work quite well, and they have generic insulin (which you can buy without a prescription in most states).

Made in the USA
Charleston, SC
16 May 2011